GETTING TO THE OTHER SIDE

DEAN RETIEF

GETTING TO THE OTHER SIDE

Expansion Strategies For An Abundant Life

Getting To The Other Side
First Edition, First Impression 2020
ISBN 978-0-620-92691-1
Copyright © Dean Retief

Published by:
Inspired Publishing
PO Box 82058 | Southdale | 2135
Johannesburg , South Africa
Email: info@inspiredpublishing.co.za
www.inspiredpublishing.co.za

© All rights are reserved. Apart from any fair dealing for the purpose of research, criticism or review as permitted under the Copyright Act, no part of this publication may be reproduced, stored in a retrieval system or transmitted, in any form or by any means, electronic, mechanical, photocopying, recording, or otherwise, without the prior written permission of the copyright holder.

TABLE OF CONTENTS

Dedication   7
Note From The Author   9
Introduction   11

CHAPTER 1   15
TAKING STOCK
Knowing where to start makes all the difference

CHAPTER 2   31
VISIONEERING
The destination makes the journey worth it

CHAPTER 3   47
MAP BUILDING
Watch out for your Programming

CHAPTER 4   63
BUILD MOMENTUM
Start small and finish strong

CHAPTER 5   77
PACK LIGHT
Letting go of the hold that others have on you

CHAPTER 6   89
PAYING YOUR OWN WAY
Your role as Steward

CHAPTER 7   105
DETOUR
When things go wrong

CHAPTER 8 117
OVERCOMING THE IMPOSSIBLE
Facing your giants

CHAPTER 9 131
GROW AS YOU GO
Personal Growth will be your portion

CHAPTER 10 145
HELPING OTHERS ALONG THE WAY
Building Strong Relationships

CHAPTER 11 157
TRUST THE MASTER NAVIGATOR
The role of the Person of the Holy Spirit

CHAPTER 12 165
GET READY FOR THE OTHER SIDE
Plan for your Expansion

DEDICATION

I would like to dedicate this book to my family- my wife, Samantha Retief, and my two daughters: Daniella and Demique Retief. Samantha has been an inspiration to my daughters and me. She lives life to the full and always reminds us that we should never settle for second best, and the importance of building and cherishing relationships. Her counsel in difficult times has been invaluable. It has helped to shape who I am today. We are celebrating our twentieth wedding anniversary during this time.

Although our two teenage daughters are gifted differently, their compassion for others and desire to make a difference in the world at such a young age is something to behold.
Some of the stories in this book are about our family. They are a reflection of what we needed to do to get to the Other Side.

TO GOD BE ALL THE GLORY!

NOTE FROM THE AUTHOR

I am forty-six years old at the time of writing this book, in the year 2020, an unprecedented year in human history, the year when the world needed to confront the Covid-19 pandemic and its social, political, financial, and economic effects. One might say the pandemic was an unexpected and unprecedented storm.

I have been through quite a few moments of transition both internally and externally and I am sure that there will be many more to come. In this book, I would like to share some principles, truths, and recipes that have helped me to navigate some of the most difficult transitions in my life. The trying aspects of my life include, **suffering from rejection and low self-esteem, addictions, becoming a husband and a dad, climbing the corporate ladder, being diagnosed with a chronic illness, saying "yes" to the call of ministry, and losing loved ones. I have lost both my father and my father-in-law; two people who were close to me. I have also had to navigate myself and my family through the Covid-19 crisis.** These are just some of the transitions I needed to navigate and some of them are still a work in progress.

I trust that my **stories and experiences will enlighten and help you** in what you might be going through and give you hope and perspective to get you to the other side. If this book instills hope in you and assures you that better days are still ahead of you, then I have done my job.

There are people in my life who have shaped who I am today. They have played the role of role models and inspired me greatly, and are a reflection of who I can become. They are teachers, instructors, obstacles that made me redirect and reflect, family, friends and companions, co-workers, bosses and corporate leaders, authors, preachers, and speakers. **I am grateful to everyone who has played a role in getting me to the other side knowingly or unknowingly on various occasions.** Getting to the other side is not a one-man job; you need good people around you who have your best interests at heart; people who speak healing and hope into your life. They are people who help you bear your burdens, or just some people who annoy you so much that you want to get to the other side just to prove them wrong or even more importantly prove yourself right. **As a man of faith, I will be reflecting on the Scriptures and the practical relevance and wisdom we can gain from it to get us to the other side. As a Masters' student of leadership and behavioral psychology,** I will tap into models and frameworks that will be of practical value for you to make the necessary shifts. Lastly, I will tap into my personal experiences and reflections that will allow you to take courage on this journey with me. **Getting to the other side might just be what you have been waiting for. You must** know that you don't have to be stagnant or be a victim of your circumstances; there are ways to overcome the obstacles of the past. New beginnings await you on the other side.

INTRODUCTION

Life always presents us with opportunities to move forward and to get to the other side of some stuff we are going through. We rarely stay at the same place or want to stay at the same place. Seasons change, time changes, and so do things within us and sometimes things around us. Life events also have an amazing surprise element of pelting you with a curve ball when you least expect it: there can be an unexpected crisis, a loss of a loved one, a disappointment you did not see coming. When such things happen, our immediate response is to ask ourselves how we can get to the other side of the obstacle or setback. How do I move forward? How do I redefine myself and make meaning out of all of this? Can I move on? Will I move on?

Somehow, an unexpected crisis reveals more about who we are at that moment than the event itself. We often need to deal with our inner crises more than what we face on the outside. When challenges confront us, we start to question certain things that we hold dear to ourselves. We ask if they will sustain us or if they are enduring. When you have decided to move on, to get to the other side, the place where you are begins to feel foreign and uncomfortable. Moving on starts to feel like a necessity and not an option. Getting to the other side starts to feel like a life or death situation. Some start to see the Promised Land -"the other side", but very few of us get there.

A scripture from the Gospel of Mark inspired the title of this book. In the scripture, Jesus requested his disciples to take a boat ride to the other side of the lake:

*Mark 4:35-41 (NIV) That day when **evening came**, he said to his disciples, **"Let us go over to the other side"**. Leaving the crowd behind, they took him along, just as he was, in the boat. There were also other boats with him. A furious squall came up, and the waves broke over the boat, so that it was nearly swamped. Jesus was in the stern, sleeping on a cushion. The disciples woke him up and said to him, "Teacher, **don't you care if we drown?"** He got up, rebuked the wind and said to the waves, "Quiet! Be still!" Then the wind died down and it completely calmed. And he said to his disciples, **"Why are you so afraid? Do you still have no faith?***

The lessons we can take out of this passage are:

1. Going to the other side does not depend on what you can see with your physical eyes; the vision will have to come from somewhere else especially if you are travelling in the evening.
2. You will always have to leave the "crowd" behind and only take with you the trusted few to the other side.
3. You will have to learn to ride the storm and fight the fear, and not to fight the storm and ride the fear.
4. You will have to protect your most valuable belongings during a storm.
5. Your growth in faith guarantees your Other Side; it will allow you to grab hold of it.
6. Make sure you have Jesus in your boat.
7. Taking a nap will prepare you for the Other Side. Jesus took a nap as he was preparing himself for another encounter on the Other Side.

During the course of this book, I will be taking you on a journey to the Other Side. I will be getting you to grips with where you are right now, defining where you would like to go, defining your road map to the other side, and getting you there. Get ready for the journey of a lifetime. If you allow it, it will be a life-transforming journey indeed.

Chapter 1

TAKING STOCK

KNOWING WHERE TO START WILL MAKE ALL THE DIFFERENCE

But when he came to himself, he said, "How many of my father's hired servants have bread enough and to spare, and I perish in hunger." – Luke 15:17

TAKING STOCK

Today we are spoiled to drive around with Google Maps navigating the way. I am not sure if you are like me. When I go to a new place, I follow the Google Maps navigator without even looking around me for landmarks just in case I get lost. I wholly trust the directions that it gives me without any reservation or asking questions. Google Maps gets me to my destination, the Other Side. It was funny one morning when my phoned died on my way to an important meeting and I needed to pull off not knowing where I was. I needed to get my phone working before I could continue with my journey.

Google Maps works on two basic principles, **it needs to know where you are, and where you would like to go. This is the truth about Google Maps and it is the truth about your life.** You cannot make an effort to get to the Other Side unless you take a hard look at where you are today. Where are you now? What season are you in? What time is it for your life? Have you noticed that Google Maps will not work if it cannot pick up your current location?

Taking stock of your life can be a daunting and sometimes painful process. Taking stock is sometimes thrown at you due to things, **people, and circumstances that are beyond your control.** The unfaithfulness of a partner or spouse, the death of a loved one, the loss of a business or retrenchment at work can leave you vulnerable and lost. Sometimes our own deeds, for example, our unfaithfulness or wrong business decisions have brought us to a place of despair or re-evaluation. Whatever the case may be, **it is what it is.**

How you take stock of where you are today is important, if not more important than where you want to go. We rarely take the time to understand what is happening to us, within us, and through us or what we need to let go of or to take with us for us to make the journey to the Other Side. There comes a time in your life that brings you to a place where you "come to yourself" to gain perspective of who you are, or who you have become, what you have become, how God sees you, how other people see you and what the condition of your own heart is. **When we move hastily, we are bound to repeat the mistakes of the past,** or carry with us the disappointment of the present that will make the journey unbearable and sometimes even impossible.

How do I take stock? Just like the prodigal son in Luke 15, **you would need three perspectives for you to move forward into the future. Firstly,** you need to get the perspective of **your heavenly Father;** He is like the satellite in the sky. He sits with a broad and perfect perspective about you. He has enough reroute capacity (grace) within Him to get you to your destination. The number of detours we sometimes take do not scare or disappoint Him, however, He is not pleased when we find our way using the easiest and shortest routes to our other side. The shortest route to the Other Side is rarely the best route as our reroutes are designed for us to let go of our unnecessary baggage. Sometimes God Himself is the architect of the reroute. Exodus 13:17-18 reminds us that God made the Israelites take the long way for their own benefit and safety on their way to the Promised Land. A two-week journey from Egypt to the Promised Land took the Israelites forty years.

Secondly, you **will need to do a non-judgmental introspection** of where you find yourself today. "Non-judgemental" is the key word.

TAKING STOCK

Blaming God, others, or yourself for where you find yourself today may sometimes be necessary to give voice to your emotional baggage; however, you cannot stay there for too long.

Dealing with the facts of a situation from an honest and outside-in view will go a long way in helping you to pinpoint your location with accuracy. The prodigal son expressed it like this: "I perish in hunger." **Maturity is not the absence of making wrong decisions in life, but owning those decisions, learning from them, and making better decisions going forward.** When it is time to take stock, you need to be clear where you are, what you have lost and gained, and what you will need to find closure on and move forward. Be aware of the emotional connections that you have made during this time. Both constructive and unconstructive emotional connections have served you in some way or form. **Unconstructive emotional connections will blur your view of who you are and will always bring you to a place of being lesser or even to a place of being a victim.**

When you continue reading the parable of the prodigal son, he comes to a place where he changes his identity from being a son to being a servant. When you are in the middle of a crisis, be careful how you name things or even more importantly, what you name yourself. Failing in a business venture or a marriage does not make you a failure. Being addicted to a substance does not make your an addict, but will make you someone who struggles with an addiction. Labelling yourself a failure will have dire consequences on how you will see the world and what you will continue to attract into your life.

Thirdly, you would need one more data point to complete your stock taking process and confirming your place of location: **the feedback you receive from others. You need to get to a place where you surround yourself with people you trust, people who can see your potential and give you honest feedback on where you are.** You need mirrors and helpers in your life during your stock taking process. Choose them wisely.

GETTING TO THE OTHER SIDE

It is quite interesting to observe that during a crisis our emotions wreak havoc within us and reveal the beliefs we hold and we reach wrong conclusions about what God thinks about us, what we think about ourselves or other people. It is only when the prodigal son arrived back home, the place that was part of his inheritance and saw the reaction of his Father, that he realised that his **starting point was very different from his destination**. Sometimes where we need to start from is not pretty. Dealing with the brutal facts of our situation does not always fill us with optimism and excitement; however, sometimes we need to admit that it is just what it is.

The following scripture reaffirms the above:

> *1. I will stand my watch and set myself on the rampart, and watch to see what He will say to me, And what I will answer when I am corrected. 2. The Lord answered me and said: "Write the vision and make it plain on tablets, That they may run who reads it. 3. For the vision as yet for an appointed time; But at the end it will speak, and it will not lie, Though it tarries wait for it; Because it will surely come: It will not tarry - Habakkuk 2:1-3*

Habakkuk also reminds us of the three perspectives that we must be equipped with when we need to take stock which are: **God's perspective** - "what He will say to me", **my own perspective** - "what I will answer", and **others' perspective** - "that they may run". Habakkuk adds two more elements that are key to taking stock. The first is writing things down and the time and season you find yourself in, because context is king. The second is **doing the right thing at the wrong time, and doing the wrong thing at the right time.** Therefore, timing is everything. Seasons and time are natural sequences of events providing opportunities to be and doing certain things that will produce the biggest return on time, energy, and resources invested.

Habakkuk also reminds us of the **importance of writing things down or some might even call it journaling. Journaling** has this amazing ability of revealing what is in your heart. This is true for taking stock as it is for casting a vision of your desired future. I will dwell more on the importance of casting a vision over your life in the next few chapters. Habakkuk also encourages us to **use all our senses as we take stock**: What did you hear? What did you see? What did you say? How did you feel "writing it on the tablets of your heart"? What did you believe ("it will speak and it will not lie"), and what did you do?

Ecclesiastes 3 puts it as follows: "To everything there is a season, and a time to every purpose under heaven...**Season, time, and purpose to everything**. I am sure that this does not refer to everything, but to the big ticket items that will shape the destiny of our lives, therefore, **what season do you find yourself in? What time is it for you**? In answering these questions, don't be surprised that some of the things that you are going through are normal and seasonal in nature. It might relate to the life or career stage that you are in, the normal effects of trauma or loss, the cause of changes in your external circumstances. This includes your relationships that will make you re-evaluate your beliefs, values, and contributions that you need to make moving forward. Maybe you are wondering to what end you need to go through all of this. Why is stocktaking so important? Can't I just continue with life and go with the flow? Take life as it comes, one day at a time and make the best of what life presents you with on a day-to-day basis. Getting to live a life to its fullest potential comes with this ever-longing feeling of fulfillment, satisfaction, flow, achievement, and meaning which all of us crave for. **Stocktaking creates the opportunity for us to evaluate how far we have come and what opportunities still exist now and in the future to make an even greater contribution.**

The Bible speaks about Christ's journey in the following way: *"Jesus grew in wisdom and stature and in favour with God and all people"* - Luke 2:52 (NLT). It is interesting to note that the three perspectives needed to confirm your location are back in play: God's perspective, Jesus's perspective and other people's perspective. This gave Jesus a confirmation of where he was on his journey. **This verse however highlights the most important outcome of the stocktaking process, taking stock of our "personal growth".** Personal development is the capacity that you create to attract things that you need to fulfil the assignment over your life. **Wisdom development refers to the quality of your thinking underpinned by sound beliefs and values, and the quality of your choices based on well-managed emotions, experience, and Godly intuition that enables you to make sense of the world around you. Stature development has all to do with you developing your presence, impact, influence, authenticity, and character as a person.** All of this contributed to Jesus gaining a better understanding of His assignment here on earth. In addition, it made him build strong and deep relationships with people around him that he needed to support his mission.

Let me get back to you and I. We can easily be tempted to take stock of our lives looking at our external achievements and failures. While to a certain extent we should not shy away from objectively looking at it, for record sake, we should not underestimate what personal growth took place during our times of failure. **Taking stock of the personal growth that took place during times of failure will set us up for future success.** We have to discard the perception that failure is a bad thing. **Success comes from learning what not to do through multiple failures.** There will be no success without failure. Taking a personal growth stance on your stocktaking process will help you to be less judgmental about where you find yourself today, so take stock of what is important to you, what you value, what the long-held beliefs are that you hold that are enabling you or stifling you. Moreover, evaluate your past choices which once set you back and why they did. Which relationships with things and people are helping you and which ones are hindering you? How far are you with the God-given assignment? Currently, where do you experience flow and favour in your life? It is time to take out the golden nuggets of where you find yourself today and continue to move forward.

Not taking stock can bring you to a place of embarrassment brought about by incomplete projects and unfulfilled dreams. We can however **not deny the fact that our lives are interrelated**, that the parts make up the sum, and some parts are more important than others. While some parts that we neglect today may not affect us, they will lead to our downfall in the long-term.

> In Luke 14:28-29 Jesus says, *"Suppose one of you wants to build a tower. Won't you first sit down and estimate the cost to see if you have enough money to complete it? For if you lay the foundation and are not able to finish it, everyone who sees it will ridicule you."* - (NIV)

Life is sometimes like a building project, you need to focus on different aspects to get the project done and more importantly, you need to be clear about the financial backing, the focus and support that you'll require to finish it on time. **All areas of your life need to contribute to where you are going-** the walls, the roof, the floor, the windows, the plumbing, and so on. While all these aspects are important, **the foundation of your building project needs to be stable** and enduring enough to build upon. If you don't have an enduring *why you do what you do* you will soon run out of steam or come to a place where you have achieved so much and still feel empty and dissatisfied. Why do you do what you do? *Whatever the answer;* why is that important to you? Will it get you closer to the foundation upon which you need to build your life? Now you can take stock of how **your family and marriage, your finances, your physical, mental and emotional health, your career, your skills and education, your social and business relationships, your spiritual life contribute or derail you from living out your big WHY.** These aspects are all important to focus on and to resource to get your building project complete.

GETTING TO THE OTHER SIDE

As we go about our stocktaking process, we soon come to the realisation that some stuff we are dealing with has nothing to do with us. It has been nurtured into us; inherited, transferred, passed on from one generation to the other. The book of Chronicles puts it as follows:

> 1 Chronicles 4:9-10; *"And Jabez was more honorable than his brethren: and his mother called his name Jabez saying, Because I bare him with sorrow. And Jabez called on the God of Israel, saying, Oh that thou wouldest bless me indeed, and enlarge my coast.*

Some of us are walking around with labels that others have placed on us from an early age. Some of us are just born into things and it is not our fault. However, the labels that we carry have a **profound impact on who we are and how we behave**. Just like Jabez, we need to be aware of these things before we move forward. You need to know **your family history** of addiction, abuse, lack, neglect, gender, and racial identity, divorce, and religious patterns of thinking that have brought pain to your life. It is important to know these to determine if history is not repeating itself. Like Jabez, these things will keep you small. Becoming **aware of them will provide you with the opportunity to break free from them.**

As we conclude this chapter on stocktaking, we need to emphasise that stocktaking is not only a painful and constructive process. This is a process you need to embark on when things are falling apart, when you are facing a crisis, and when certain things are ending and you need to move to the next phase of your life. **Taking stock when your life is on the up and up will set you up for expansion.** This is true for your life as it is for your business or organisation.

> Matthew 25:20-21 *"And he who had received the five talents came forward, bringing five talents more, saying 'Master, you delivered to me five talents; here, I have made five talents more. His master said to him, Well done, good and faithful servant. You have been faithful*

*over little, I will set you over much. Enter into
the joy of your Master. (ESV)*

Getting to **success recipes** in certain parts of your life **can be replicated in other areas** to bring about expansion. The concept of franchising is a great example of this. One successful store can be replicated to bring about expansion. It only takes one "faithful" store that delivers the **desired return for success to be expanded**. So as part of your stock taking process **look at your past successes** and see how you can expand it even further into other parts of your life.

"GETTING YOU TO THE OTHER SIDE" GROWTH PLAN

Stocktaking Mastery

The time has come for us to get practical regarding where you find yourself today, right now. Stocktaking is such an important process, because **your current location will be invaluable for you to set a course to get you to the other side**. As I mentioned before, you would need three perspectives to get you going; **God's perspective, your perspective, and the perspective of others. Self-awareness is always half the battle won to get you to the Other Side.** Depending on where you find yourself, this process can be daunting, so take your time, write things down, and pray for the process as you go along. Write down what comes to your mind during this process. You will have ample time to revisit this exercise as you continue on this journey.

GETTING TO THE OTHER SIDE

LET'S PRAY

Dear heavenly Father, I believe that this is a God-ordained moment for me to take stock of my life. I stand in agreement that the time has come for me to get to other side of a few things in my life. I pray that you bring into remembrance the things I need to look at. As daunting as that might be, I know that you will never leave nor forsake me. Nothing that I will confess or make known will surprise You, because You were there all the time. You know every part of my history and my inner-being and You love me just the same. In Jesus Name. Amen

GETTING A PERSPECTIVE ON THE TIME AND SEASON

1. When you look over your life **which season** do you find yourself in? Is it **Winter, Spring, Summer, or Autumn?** Why is that so? What season comes after the season that you are in? What does that mean to you? What role does your age and stage in life play?

2. What do you do at this time of your life? What is **important to you now**? What do you need to leave behind and let go of? What do you **need to take with you** to the Other Side?

With the above in mind, it is important that you explore how all other areas of your life are **interrelated** and how they have contributed to bringing you to the place, time, and season in which you find yourself today.

TAKING STOCK

YOUR HISTORY WITH FAMILY, RELATIONSHIPS AND THINGS

1. What are the **stand out moments of your home-life** and your upbringing? What are the **painful moments of your home-life** and upbringing? How has both positively and negatively impacted your life and the way you see life?
2. Think about your **most impactful relationships** over your lifetime so far, both positive and negative. How have they **shaped who you** are today?
3. What **"things" are you connected to**, both good and bad? How have they helped you to both **cope and thrive** in where you are today?
4. What has been your family **view about God**, how has this **helped you or hindered** you in how you see Him?
5. How would you rate the quality of your own family or home right now out of ten? Why that rating?
6. List all the **important relationships** that you have with people or things. Label each relationship **with a negative or positive**. What does that say about the relationships you have?

YOUR PERSONAL SPIRITUAL, PHYSICAL, EMOTIONAL, AND MENTAL WELL-BEING

1. How would you **rate your spiritual well-being**, your ability to give yourself to a cause bigger than yourself in service to others, **out of 10?** Why that score?
2. How would you **rate your mental well-being**, your ability to think through things and respond appropriately to the challenges of life, **out of 10?** Why that score?
3. How would you rate your **emotional well-being**, your ability to manage your emotions that you are able to respond appropriately to people around you, **out of 10?** Why that score?
4. How would you rate your **physical well-being**, your eating and sleeping patterns, habits, your exercise and weight, that provide you with enough energy to tackle most days, **out of 10?** Why that score?

5. How much **time, effort, and resources** do you spend on the things **that you really love to do?**
6. When you reflect on your **overall well-being?** What does it say about where you find yourself today? How does this tie up with the feedback that you are receiving from those you trust?

HISTORY WITH FINANCE, CAREER, AND CAPABILITIES

1. What is your current **relationship with money?** How does that help or hinder you?
2. Do you know what you are good at and are you growing in it? Does it create the necessary **financial stability** that you need?

IT IS TIME TO PACK YOUR BAGS FOR YOUR JOURNEY TO THE OTHER SIDE

For this journey, you will have three compartments in your bag. **Compartment One: things that you definitely want to take with you (positive), Compartment Two: things that you have to work on (positive/negative), and Compartment Three: things that you have to discard (negative).**

As you reflect on the stocktaking process and journalling, what are the things that you must take with you on this journey? Make a list.

What are the things that need to change? This includes things that are within your control and are part of the journey that you would like to focus on.

What are the things you need to let go of, at this time, to lighten the burden and the weight of your bag?

TAKING STOCK

What are the things that I would like to take with me? (+)	What are things that I would like to change as part of my journey?(-/+)	What are things that I would like to let go of as part of my journey? (-)
1. What I believe is important to me. 2. The time and season that I am in. 3. Things in my life that are working, that I can build on. 4. Lessons I have learned along the way that can help me on this journey. 5. Things that I am grateful for.	1. Getting better at certain things that will help me to move forward. 2. The things I need to change to move to my next season.	1. Past pains and disappointments that are keeping me boxed in 2. Removing the unhealthy and unwanted labels of the past. 3. Connections to things, beliefs, emotions, and people who stall my progress.

You have packed your bags and you are ready to go. Don't be surprised that you may need to do some repacking as you embark on this journey; more things will come to your mind.

It is time to take some spiritual vitamins for the journey.

"Being confident of this very thing, that He who has begun a good work in you will complete it until the day of Jesus Christ"
Phillipians 1:6

"Therefore we also, since we are surrounded by so great a cloud of witnesses, let us lay aside every weight, and the sin that so easily ensnares us, and let us run with endurance the race that is set before us, looking unto Jesus the author and finisher of our faith"-
Hebrews12:1-2 (NKJV)

"Cast all your anxiety on Him because He cares for you" -
1 Peter 5:17

GETTING TO THE OTHER SIDE

"For God has not given us the. spirit of fear, but of power, and love and a sound mind "- 2 Tim 1:7 (NKJV)

God the great navigator is on your side. Enjoy the rest of your Journey.

LET'S PRAY

Dear heavenly Father, thank you for being with me through this stocktaking process. I see what You see, and I can hear what You want to show me. Thank you for taking me through the seasons of my life. I continue to request your guidance and support as I venture on. In Jesus name, I pray Amen.

Chapter 2
VISIONEERING

THE DESTINATION MAKES THE JOURNEY WORTH IT!

"Looking unto Jesus the author and finisher of our faith, who for the joy that was set before him endured the cross, despising the shame, and is set down at the right hand of the throne of God – Hebrews 12:2 (NKJV)

There is nothing in life that inspires one to make the necessary sacrifices more than the prospect of a better tomorrow or a brighter future. **We can handle the pain if we are clear about the gain.** Just as it is important to know where you are now, you need to be clear about where you want to go. **Direction focuses the mind** and your resources to move you in the direction of your destination. Setting a picture of a desired future cannot come from a half-hearted place, but in most cases it stems from a personal place with deep emotional connection that, once achieved, will make your life and the lives of others around you better.

An unfulfilled vision in your heart is more agonising than the process or journey that you need to take to accomplish it, therefore a vision is not what you see with your eyes, but what you desire within your heart. A vision is a heart condition, not a head condition.

The book of Nehemiah puts it as follows:

Therefore, the king said to me, "Why is your face sad, since you are not sick? This is nothing but the sorrow of the heart." So I became dreadfully afraid, and said to the king, "May the king live forever! Why should my face not be sad, when the city, the place of my fathers' tombs, lies waste, and its gates are burned with fire?" Then the king said to me, "what do you request?" So I prayed to the God of heaven, And I said to the king, "If it pleases the king, and if your servant has found favor in your sight, I ask that you send me to Judah, to the city of my fathers' tombs, that I may rebuild it." - Nehemiah 2:1-5 (NKJV)

Being unhappy with something and **wanting to change it for the benefit of others is a good breeding ground for a vision.** Sharing what is in your heart, with the right people, at the right time, will attract support from unexpected sources. Nehemiah also reminds us that God wants a heartfelt vision, a vision that sees others being restored from a place of compassion and deep conviction. **Vision requires you to dig deep** and at the same time for you to be on the outlook for opportunities that will propel it forward. Every vision that you cast will require your full commitment and involvement to accomplish it. The pain and disappointment we sometimes sit with about things that should change in our lives will sometimes become the driving force that gets us up in the morning in pursuit of a brighter day or a better tomorrow, our reason for being. Like Nehemiah, a vision can relate to fixing things from the past, things that will impact your present, and set the tone or new foundations for generations to come. A **vision has a lot to do with leaving a legacy behind.**

Proverbs 29:18(KJV) puts it like this *"Where there is no vision, people perish, but he that keepeth the law, happy is he.*

Vision is not what you see with your eyes, but what is revealed in your heart. This revelation sheds light on what is already in your heart, to be and to do, and without this revelation, you either remain stagnant or waste your time, being and doing what is not in your design. Perishing refers something or someone who has huge potential, but wastes it due to a lack of direction. The book of Proverbs also reminds us that there are certain laws, rules, principles, and recipes that govern this process, and that both **the revelation of a vision and the pursuit thereof will bring you to a place of fulfillment**.

However, we need to be aware that a vision is revelational in nature. You start with what you know to be true for now, but expect that God will provide more clarity along the way.

So where does a vision come from? Psalm 37:4 (NKJV) says, *"Delight yourself also in the Lord, and He shall give you the desires of your heart."* It is reassuring to know that the same God who gives you insight during your stocktaking process, is the same God who will show you where to go if you seek His face. The Psalmist reminds us that **God gives the "desires",** so the desires that you sit with to make different areas of your life better, in service towards others, are mostly God-given. This compels God since He has given you these desires, to provide the necessary resources and support so that He can give you the desires of your heart. **For every God-given vision, there will be a God-given provision.**

Our biggest challenge in life is pursuing someone else's vision, claiming it to be our own. We are bombarded, on a daily basis, with input from people and things around us regarding who we ought to be, what we ought to be, how we ought to be that we sometimes find it very difficult to find our own authentic voice to hear the voice of our "hearts' desires". **Vision is a heart condition that is translated and visualised in the mind.** A vision that starts in the mind, based on what you see others do, or in comparison to what others do, will lack conviction and commitment from the heart. While it will work for a while, it will quickly run out of steam and ultimately die unfulfilled.

Romans 12:2 (NKJV) And do not be conformed to this to this world, but be transformed by the renewing of your mind, that you may prove what is that good and acceptable and perfect will of God."

Taking on the shape to conform to something or someone else's vision, based on what you see going on around you, will take you further from who you need to be. Comparing yourself with others will just impose unrealistic, self-limiting beliefs and expectations on you. Why do you want to be like someone else if you can be the best version of yourself? A God-given vision is good, acceptable and perfect just for you, but requires a shift in your thinking to embrace it. I will speak more about this in the chapters to come, because to accomplish your vision, a reprogramming of your mind will be required. A **vision will probably be one of the most powerful transformative processes in your life.**

So what is a vision? Habakkuk chapter 2 is probably the most profound revelation on a Vision.

> *"I will stand my watch and set myself on a rampart, and watch to see what He will say to me, and what I will answer when I am corrected. Then the Lord answered me and said, "Write the vision and make it plain on tablets, that he may run who reads it. For the vision is yet for an appointed time, but at the end it will speak, and it will not lie. Though it tarries, wait for it because it will surely come, it will not tarry. Behold the proud, his soul is not upright in him; but the just shall live by his faith." - Habakkuk 2:1- 4 (NKJV)*

Some of the important principles about a vision from this these verses are:

1. Distance yourself from your current surroundings to **start "dreaming" again**. You need a space where you can listen to your heart again.
2. Talk to God about this, and whatever He is saying to you; you need to start to picture it. **"See what He will say."**
3. Make yourself vulnerable before Him so that He can **test the intentions of your heart and strip you of your limiting beliefs that are** based on your past experiences and programming.
4. Be ready to **write things down** so that they can become a mirror of **what is going on in your heart.**
5. Don't be fancy or think about other people and what they might say; **make it plain.** What do you **want to see?** What does that

mean to you? **Who will you become** in the process, **how will this serve** and benefit others? What will you need in this process? A vision captures your heart and involves all your senses to see the opportunities for evolvement and fulfillment.
6. The clearer the vision, the more support you will attract for its accomplishment- **"he may run who reads it."**
7. You must **set a timeline; a realistic one**, so that your vision does not lie. In most cases, we are talking about a three to five-year-plan. **Visions will have an appointed time, a date of completion,** as times and seasons change. However, "who" you are and **your purpose in life will remain the same.**
8. Once you have settled this vision in your heart, be on the **outlook for various opportunities** that will come your way to fulfill it.
9. Your own **self-sufficiency (pride) will be your biggest stumbling block** to getting you to your vision. You will soon realise that **your vision is bigger than you,** and needs you to live by faith to see it through. **Faith also brings the three to five-plan into the here and now so that you can see the opportunities and provision provided for it daily. You need to live for your vision daily (live by faith), not work for it, but work with and on it.**

We should not downplay the importance that your faith will play in your vision. Without faith, there can be no vision, because a **vision is a result of the expression of your faith**. Faith allows you to see the invisible future with all its possibilities, even in the midst of impossibilities.

According to Hebrews 11:1(NKJV) "Now faith is the substance of things that you hoped for, the evidence of things not seen."

Here are some pointers that we find about the importance of faith. They will be very beneficial as we cast a vision over our lives.

1. **Faith brings the picture of the future into the here and now,** so that you can see the opportunities and provisions for its

accomplishment on a daily basis.
10. **Faith brings substance**, **real depth, meaning**, evidenceand **tangible expectations** to your vision. It is possible. Is this true of your vision?
11. **Faith enables you to draw pictures in your head**, stemming from your heart, of a brighter future that **instills hope and optimism.**
12. **Faith overrides** the "things seen", **the impossibilities** of the now, and **presents you** with the various **possibilities of the future** "the unseen".
13. Faith allows you to **co-create your desired future.**
14. **Faith functions on substance and evidence,** just like natural logic, however the only difference is that it functions on the "unseen" and not the "seen", therefore **faith can be defined as supernatural logic, based on substance and evidence. It brings the future into the now.**
15. Faith is all about bringing your desired future into the here and now. However, you have to bring the One who holds the future, God Himself, to your here and now, to see what He has in store for you.

It is quite sad to observe how we live without visions, or sometimes with half-baked or half-hearted views of our desired futures. No wonder we receive half-baked provisions and opportunities. As I alluded in the stocktaking chapter, we need three perspectives to understand where we are today, as well as where we need to go. What does God have to say around the shifts that you require to take you forward? What do you have to say about your desired future? What feedback have you received from others that confirms and brings greater insights about your next destination? **Visioneering should not be a once off process, but needs to be worked with and worked on. Because a vision is a revelational process, it becomes clearer as you move along, and the clearer it gets, the more opportunities will present themselves for its fulfillment.**

A LESSON FROM A LETTER

At the time of writing this book I stumbled across a letter that I wrote to myself more than 15 years ago; when I was 30 years old to be precise. I projected what I would love to have in my life five to ten years from then. I knew that I had done this, but I could not remember the details of the letter. What I am about to share with you will just boggle your mind. During that time of my live I had so many insecurities and struggles going on in my mind, but I had deep desires in my heart that I could not shake off. That must have been desires that were placed there by God himself. Before I share the contents of the letter with you, I need to remind you that you should not allow the current circumstances of your life to stop you from envisioning a better and brighter future. Not something far-fetched, but dreams that comes from an authentic place that you know is part of your destiny here on earth.

Because the letter wasn't written in a typical format and really just looks like scribbles on a piece of paper, I couldn't include it here for you to see, but I have extracted the content and included here in point form. I will break it down point by point and give you an extract from the letter, followed by some context about my reality at the time and then show you how that has translated into my current experience.

Here we go…

Letter: "I am glad to be alive and God has been God to me and my family. My wife and my two children are experiencing life to the fullest. Our children are well balanced, gifted in their own right and emotionally mature. We have travelled the world and we are living an independent and debt free life"

Context: At the time of writing this letter we had only one child. We had never travelled overseas. Our marriage was taking serious strain and we were about to lose everything we had.

Today: We have two teenage children who are gifted, well balanced and emotionally matured. Our marriage and our family has never been better. We have travelled all over the world in the past ten years and we are financially independent.

Letter: "My wife runs a legal counseling firm and an early childhood development business, while busy influencing and developing new leaders and my private business is thriving"

Today: We are proud owners of three Early Childhood Development (ECD) Centres and an ECD College. I left the Corporate world not too long ago to start the Leadership Development Firm and it is starting to show great promise. Not quite sure about the legal counseling firm?

Letter: "We are Pastoring a 2500 member Church that is authentic and highly purpose-driven. We are the new kids on the block. Our marriage is a great example and we are sharing our life lessons through marriage seminars; restoring many."

Context: At this time we were a very small and insignificant Church. We were about to enter a season where we would experience a major break in the Church. Our marriage was about to face one of its biggest challenges that would almost cost us our marriage.

Today: We are one of the fastest growing churches in our community and we are well on our way to growing to a 2500 member church face-to-face and online. The core calling of the church is to connect people to their God-given purpose, destiny and design. Over the past three years we have had the privilege of conducting numerous marriage seminars, impacting and restoring many marriages.

Letter: "We own various properties; three to be precise, including a farm. We are driving SUV's and have millions in our bank accounts. My wife looks as stunning as ever - matured and well balanced. I have taken up golf."

Context: At the time we only had one property, owned two sedans and had a few thousand Rands in our bank account. I definitely was not playing golf at the time!

Today: Today we are proud owners of six properties that includes a farm. We reached millionaire status in our mid-thirties and my wife competed in the finals of the Mrs. South Africa pageant and won the Most Empowered Women Award for that year. Staying on a golf estate has given me no option but to take up the game of golf.

Letter: "I am in the process of writing my first book and I am being invited as a guest speaker at various functions, both locally and internationally."

Context: At the time there was no book in the pipeline. I had other major issues to deal with.

Today: This book is a fulfillment of that desire. Can you believe that? More than fifteen years in the making. God will surely give you the desires of your heart.

What am I trying to show you? Even I under-estimated the power of vision. Making it plain and writing it down. Sharing the above is not to show what I have accomplished, but to show you not to be afraid to make your desires known. There is power in a God-ordained vision!

A picture of this letter is available as an annexure at the end of the book

"GETTING YOU TO THE OTHER SIDE"
GROWTH PLAN
Visioneering Mastery

LET'S PRAY

"Dear heavenly Father, thank you for blessing me with the desire for a better future. Allow me during this time to dig deeper into my heart so that I can see what you have to say about me. You have not given me the spirit of fear, but of acceptance, that it is ok to dream again from a place of non-judgement, and with an earnest desire to please You and serve others, and in turn discover who I need to be in the process. Continue to reveal to me the layers of this vision and bring clarity to my mind about what I need to work with and to work on.
In Jesus name. Amen

THE VISIONEERING PROCESS:

STEP 1: Find a quiet place where you can spend the next forty-five minutes alone and uninterrupted. Have your book and pen ready. Play some soft soothing music in the background. Pray the above prayer.

STEP 2: Read over the stocktaking exercise notes of the previous chapter. Take note of the things that you really want to change moving forward. Make notes around the shifts that you need to make from where you are today to where you want to be in the future.

STEP 3: Document why these shifts would be important to God, to yourself and to others around you. See yourself making these shifts. What will be the gain if you achieve these shifts? What will be the pain if you don't? I trust that after you have made this list, and you are clear that this vision is worth pursuing.

STEP 4: The time has come for you to bring your future into the now. I would like you to write a letter to yourself. You can either use a three or a five-year timeline, so on top of the page write down the date, three or five years from now. Start the letter with Dear (Your Name). You need to write the letter in the present tense (bring the future into the now), Where are you? What are you busy doing? What have you achieved? Who have you become? What do you see? What do you smell? How do you feel? With the shifts that you wanted to make done and dusted, who have you become and how does that benefit others? Keep on writing whatever flows from the heart. Watch out for your limiting beliefs judging you. Use your heart to think. Don't allow your mind to think; it will limit you. Include all the areas of your life, your family life, your career, your finances, and your relationships.

STEP 5: Picture that this date has come and everything that you wrote down has been fulfilled. How do you feel about that? Thank God in advance for His provision.

STEP 6: Commit to reading this letter to yourself over the next three weeks, so that it can confirm what is in your heart. Get yourself ready to run with it.

Just like Nehemiah, **don't share this vision with anyone.** The issues of the heart are sacred and you should protect them. Don't let this note lie around. As you go on this journey, you will only share bits of your vision with individuals that you believe are able to help and support you to accomplish different parts of your vision. You will soon discover that **your main role**, as the visioneer, **will be to work with and on your vision and to protect your heart from attacks** that may nullify it. Don't forget that a **vision is revelational in nature**; you will have to come back and modify it as God provides more clarity along the way.

For now enjoy the butterflies flying around in your stomach, because life is about to get better. Your **destination has a picture** and it is a compelling one. Now that you have a strong indication of what you want, watch out for opportunities that you have missed or ignored before. They will become available for you to achieve your vision. In addition, be on the outlook for like-minded people that will be a great resource to help you along the way. Watch how your prayer life changes and becomes more focused, shifting from asking to thanking Him for the open doors and opportunities.

It's time for more vitamins for our journey ahead.

> "For I know the plans I have for you," says the Lord. "They are plans for good and not for disaster, to give you a future and a hope" - Jeremiah 29:11

> "For we are God's workmanship, created in Christ Jesus for good works, which He prepared beforehand that we should walk in it." - Ephesians 2:10 (KJV)

> "As a man thinks in his heart, so is he" - Proverbs 23:7

> "But let patience have it's perfect work, that you may be perfect and complete, lacking nothing" - James 1:4 (NKJV)

Let's close this important chapter.

LET'S PRAY

Dear heavenly Father, thank you for filling my life with hope, as you start to reveal the plans you have for me. I thank you in advance and I commit my obedience to be actively involved in pursuing the opportunities you provide for the fulfillment of this vision. I will work on and with this vision as I protect my heart against attacks and distractions. In Jesus name. Amen

Chapter 3

MAP BUILDING

WATCH OUT FOR YOUR PROGRAMMING

Do not conform to the pattern of this world, but be transformed by the renewing of your mind. Then you will be able to test and approve what God's will is–his good, pleasing and perfect will - Romans 12:2 (NIV)

MAP BUILDING

A dream without a plan can quickly turn into a nightmare. However, doing things the same way you have always done them will probably give you the same results. So, before we make and put down physical plans, **we need to interrogate the maps in our minds.** Trying to solve life problems with the same thinking that created them, will make you to go nowhere fast.

The book of Romans reminds us that we can easily **operate out of habit enabled by patterns of thinking** that have been ingrained in us due to our past. This brings us to a place where the outcome is "not so good", "not so pleasing", and "not so perfect". The current pattern of this world is to conform and to fit into a specific shape based on a system that wants to restrict and make you seek the approval of others rather than seeking the approval of God.

Enlisting yourself to a **never-ending mind renewal process** is a non-negotiable commitment if you have any chance of getting to the Other Side. Nothing will change your life like you changing your mind around certain things. The transformation process that the book of Romans describes is metamorphic in nature: the caterpillar turning into the butterfly effect. **Men are unable to go where their thinking can't take them.**

So how does programming happen and how can I reprogram myself?

Firstly, we need to appreciate what needs reprogramming. It involves the renewal of your mind, **the way you think**, **the choices that you make** and **the way you feel** about yourself. A pattern is created between what you think, how you decide, and how you feel about something, an event, person, and even yourself. The **stronger the link, the stronger the pattern.** The stronger the pattern, the more predictable the outcome of your behaviour that will eventually contribute to the results or fruits in your life. So, the **results you are experiencing** in your life have a **lot to do with your programming.**

So how does this programming happen?

I would like to take you to a few passages of scripture that we will use to shed light on this question.

> *Romans 10:17 (NKJV) - So **faith comes by hearing**, and hearing by the word of God*

> *Romans 10:9 (NKJV) - If you **confess with your mouth that** Jesus is Lord, and **believe in your heart** that God has raised Him from the dead, **you will be saved.***

> *Matthew 18:19(NKJV) - Again I say unto you, that if two of **you shall agree** on earth as touching anything that they shall ask, it shall **be done for them** of my Father which is in heaven.*

> *Proverbs 22:6 (KJV) - **Train up a child** in the way he should go; and **when he is old**: he **will not depart** from it.*

We **all live by faith;** driving over a green light without looking or sitting on a chair without checking if it can carry your weight are small examples that all of us live by faith. However, whom or what we have faith in makes us different from each other. What we **believe underpins our behaviours** and attitudes. What you do and how you do things today shows what you believe in. So where does our faith come from? **Faith comes by hearing**; the voices we listen to and accept as true, play a significant role in our programming. Who and what we listen to will determine the quality of our Christian faith or any faith for that matter. Irrespective of what and whom you listen to, faith will come. Things that have been spoken over our lives since the beginning of our existence have shaped who we are today. These voices came through in **words spoken and even more so through actions,** and as the saying goes: "Actions have the ability to speak even louder than words." As we grew up, we started to believe certain things about ourselves to be true; we accepted these "truths" in our hearts, we speak them over ourselves during our inner self-talks and sometimes we are even brave enough to articulate them loudly.

Programming can only happen with your permission. Things spoken over your life need permission, **your permission or your agreement,** for them to register in your heart. This agreement happens with your active or passive participation. When someone smacks you and you say or do nothing, you are passively agreeing that what they are doing is right and you should not be surprised when it happens again. Most of our programming happens through this process when we don't speak out, because sometimes we can't or sometimes we won't.

Programming that took place during our childhood will contribute more to defining the outcomes of our lives. It is as if we were placed on **"train" tracks ("train up a child")** when we were young, and now that we are older, the scenery has changed, our context is different, but we are still on the "same train track", struggling with and overcoming the same things that will not depart from us now that we are older. This is just a startling reminder for all of us on **the importance of sound and healthy parenting.**

GETTING TO THE OTHER SIDE

So how do we start the reprogramming process?

Programming starts with you agreeing, granting permission to voices recording things on your heart. To start the reprogramming process, you will have to **break those agreements** and **make new ones** that will set the renewing of your mind process into motion.

Titus 2:11-12 (NIV) For the **grace of God** has appeared that offers salvation to all people. It **teaches us to say "No"** to ungodliness and worldly passions, and to live self-controlled, upright, and godly lives in this present age.

> *2 Corinthians 10:5 (NIV) We demolish arguments and every pretension that sets itself up against the knowledge of God, and we take captive of every thought to make it obedient to Christ.*

Breaking mental agreements of the past is the starting point of your renewal process. Saying "No" to long-held beliefs about yourself, God, and others will start to "demolish arguments" that have prevented you from living a self-controlled and fruitful life. You are going to have to learn to say "Yes" to the programming that you want, and say "No" to the destructive voices in your life.

Now that we have shed some light on how programming takes places, let us look at two different programming strategies and the respective outcomes of each:

Strategy One: Programming that starts with your feelings (emotions)

> *"Now Jabez was more honorable than his brothers, and his mother called his name Jabez, saying, because I bare him with sorrow. And Jabez called on the God of Israel, saying, Oh that You would bless me indeed, and enlarge my territory, that Your hand would be with me, and that You would keep me from evil, that I may not cause pain." So, God granted him what he requested.*
> *- 1 Chronicles 4:9-10 (NKJV)*

Labelling things especially during a **time of pain** can have a profound **impact on our lives**. Jabez realised that the **labelling of his mother** over his life would bring him to a place where he would become what she had labelled him with. He made his desire known that he would like to break free from the limitations of his past and in this case from the programming he had received from his childhood home. We cannot deny that our early **childhood experiences** have played a significant part on **how we think, decide, or feel about ourselves** today. Some of these experiences are good and some are painful. During the **painful experiences** in our lives, the "not so good", "not so pleasing", and "not so perfect" programming took place and it **has impacted our perspective** in life. In addition, it has distorted the way we see God, ourselves, and others.

Let us look at another text;

"For God knows that in the day you eat of it your eyes will be opened, and you will be like God, knowing good and evil. So when the woman saw that the tree was good for food, that it was pleasant to the eyes, and a tree desirable to make one wise, she took of its fruit and ate. She also gave to her husband, and he ate" - Genesis 3:5-6 (NKJV)

When the devil got Eve to believe that **there was something wrong with her,** that she was not wise enough, which of course was a lie, he could **put programming into motion** that would lead to her destruction. This was true for Eve then as it is true for us today. The **"feeling" of not being good enough** creates **fertile programming ground for destructive patterns of thinking**, choices and emotions. If this programming goes unchecked, it will just repeat itself in different forms, areas, and stages of our lives. In most cases, starting programming from a feelings perspective leads to destruction. Feelings are volatile, unstable, and change often; they are contextual in nature, and they are just an indicator of something deeper going on. Imagine if you built your life, your programming, on how you felt at a given point in time. Just imagine that this is based on a painful event or trauma. Whatever programming that has happened during that time will be emotionally charged, and will impact how you feel, believe, and behave today even if the context has changed.

Based on the above this is normally how these strategies work:

Strategy One

Step 1: It starts with "how" **you feel about yourself and others** given a specific event or experience (past or present) that made you feel "not good enough", "not perfect enough" and "not pleasing enough".

Step 2: It creates a pattern of thinking **about yourself and others** that connects you to that "feeling". The more painful or traumatic the event, the stronger the connection between your "feeling" and that pattern of thinking. This creates a stronghold- a deeply entrenched pattern of thinking.

Step 3: You **behave in alignment to what** you believe about yourself and others. It is not possible to behave differently to what you believe. Your pattern of thinking that you hold about yourself and others will always show, if not in your words, it will show in how you behave.

Step 4: This creates your **current reality** and **reinforces** your belief about yourself and others.

I can remember going through an eye operation at the age of six and I needed to wear a patch as well as some weird glasses for my eye to heal. With that reality came a lot of teasing and bullying from the children and teachers. That brought me to a place of feeling not "good enough", "not perfect enough" and not "pleasing enough". I soon withdrew from big crowds and I avoided girls at all costs. That became my reality; it intensified during my teenage years. This made me behave awkwardly. I overstretched myself and sought the approval

MAP BUILDING

of other people, especially friends who eventually rejected me and reinforced that I was not "good" enough. Can you imagine how this programming continued to play out in my young adult life, and how this pattern of thinking created chaos until the reprogramming journey started?

What I also discovered during this time was that I did not have my perspective and priorities straight. A programming that is based on feelings puts the perspective of others in the following order: You first care about what others think about you. This impacts on what you think about yourself which in turn creates an image of what you think God thinks about you. Programming based on feelings puts others' perspective about you first; your perspective about yourself becomes secondary, and God's comes last. You are bound by the opinions and approval of others and you will experience discomfort knowing who you are and just being who you are. Quitting this discomfort quickly leads to all types of addictions. I'll discuss this at length later in the chapter.

Strategy Two: Programming that starts with the Truth

There is nothing as liberating as living out a truth instead of a lie. There is something powerful behind building your life on something authentic, noble and real. You are just free to be authentically you, making no excuses for who you are, but making a difference and leaving a mark wherever you go. This might be different for different stages of your life; however, at every stage of your life you are present and ready to take on the world. You are ready to learn, grow and flourish, but this does not happen by chance; it happens by showing that you are willing to change; it happens by design and deliberate programming. The following few verses give us amazing insight into this process:

Philipians 4:8-9 (MSG) - Summing it all up, I'd say you'll do best by

filling your minds *and meditating on things* ***true, noble, reputable, authentic, compelling, gracious - the best,*** *not the worst;* ***the beautiful,*** *not the ugly;* ***things to praise,*** *not things to curse.* ***Put into practice*** *what you learned from me, what you heard and saw and realized. Do that, and God, who makes everything work together, will work you into his* ***most excellent*** *harmonies.*

John 8:32 (NIV) - Then you will ***know the truth,*** *and the truth will* ***set you free.***

James 1:6-8(NKJV) But let him ask in faith, with no doubting, for he who doubts is like a wave of the sea driven and tossed by the wind. For let not that man suppose that he will receive anything from the Lord; he is a ***double-minded man, unstable in all his ways.***

Joshua 1:8(NKJV) This book of the Law shall not depart from ***your mouth,*** *but you shall* ***meditate in it day and night,*** *that you may* ***observe to do*** *according to all that is written in it. For then you will make your* ***way prosperous,*** *and then you will have* ***good success.***

There are only **two voices in this world.** One that **breaks you down** and takes you away from who you are supposed to be, and one that **builds you up** so that you can become who you are supposed to be. These two voices speak to you every day, and **you choose** the one you are going to listen to. "Filling your minds", "Knowing the Truth", and "Meditating on it day and night", are all **deliberate actions** to you being intentional **about your programming.** What you hear and what you speak over your life is important. How do you know that you have embraced the truth? The **truth works** out everything for your good; it gets you to a place where **you can be free to decide,** because freedom without choice is not freedom at all. The truth gives you **a place of stability that** you can stand on. The truth makes **your way prosperous** and gives you **good success.**

The Creator fully knows the extent and **potential of His creation.** Many people today can speak about the potential of the Apple iPhone,

MAP BUILDING

and their opinions and observations might be true; however, when Steve Jobs speaks about the iPhone, we all listen because he is the creator who truly knows the full potential of the iPhone.

Our Creator is the only who knows our full potential. When He speaks, we stand up and listen. While He will use many people around us to speak affirmation and truth into our lives, the most reliable source of the truth is His Word.

So how does this programming work?

Step 1: Whatever you are going through in life, **apply the truth of God's Word** to your situation. See the opportunity to either **grow your character, your compassion, or your competence** in that specific area of your life. What can I learn? What can I take out of this situation that will help me now and in the future?

Step 2: Allow step one to shape what you believe about God, yourself, and others. Keep the shaping in that order: **God first, you second and others last.** Make sure what you believe liberates you to make choices so that you can **respond to the situation and not just react** to it. **Deal with the facts** of the situation and determine what is going on. As you **apply the truth**, see the **opportunities for growth and change.**

Step 3: Agree in your heart to the **small actions and behaviors that align to what you believe in**. Appreciate that whatever you decide might be new to you and might even be uncomfortable, so start small, let God and yourself know that you are serious about this change. **The smaller you start,** the easier it will be for you to **manage the change**. As your **confidence grows, increase your commitment.**

Step 4: Start **acknowledging** the positive and constructive **"feelings"** that you are experiencing. You will soon discover that you **behave yourself into feeling better** about yourself and others. **Celebrate**

progress and show gratitude. If you are overwhelmed with negative emotions, go back to step 1.

"When any real progress is made, we unlearn and learn anew what we thought we knew before" - Henry Thoreau

"The illiterate of the 21st century will not be those who cannot read and write, but those who cannot learn, unlearn and relearn" - Alvin Toffler

I struggled with an addiction for more than twenty years. The more I tried to overcome it, the more I ended up failing at it. My failure brought me to a place of guilt and shame. I disappointed myself and others around me. I eventually agreed to seek help and I ended up seeing a pastoral counsellor. In the conversation, I was confronted with the idea of a broken identity that stemmed from my relationship with my father. We applied the truth to that situation and that released the burden and allowed me to see myself through God's eyes. I went through a process of forgiveness towards my father, which changed the way I saw him and myself. At the end of the session, I was wondering what my relationship with my father had to do with my addiction. I soon realised that my broken identity was the main cause of it. Applying the truth helped me to change my belief in God, my father and me pertaining to the addiction. Choice now became an option; I was no more a slave to addiction. I could now respond and not just react. As they say, the rest is history. Thank God for His Word. His word is the Truth.

"GETTING YOU TO THE OTHER SIDE"
GROWTH PLAN
Map Building Mastery

LET'S PRAY

Dear heavenly Father, I want to say thank you that You have a refreshed and renewed destination in store for me. I acknowledge and recognise that getting to the Other Side requires a new map, a new way of thinking and a change of mind. Bring to my remembrance mental programming that needs to be renewed for me to make progress to the Other Side, in Jesus name I pray. Amen

So let us get practical:

Exercise 1 (Truth-based Programming): Think about a life event that has significantly changed your life for the better;

1. What would you say God has to say about this situation?
1. What did you take out of this situation?
2. How has this impacted people around you?
3. How were you able to build on this?
4. What did you learn from this?

Exercise 2 (Feelings- based Programming): Think about a life event that has significantly impacted your life for the worse:

1. How did people make you feel during that time?
5. How has that impacted how you feel about yourself today?
6. Where was God in all of this?

7. What things can't you do today because of this?
8. What do you take out of this?

The exercises above clearly differentiate between truth-based programming and feelings-based programming. We have many feelings-based programmes running through our system that have been limiting us in small and big ways. It is time to say "No"! When you say "no" to something you are disagreeing with in your current state of affairs, you are inviting new ways of thinking to flood and renew your mind. A higher level of thinking, a different map- a better way becomes available to you. If you apply the truth-based programming to your feelings-based programming, your reprogramming journey starts.

Exercise 3: Go back and read the letter that we wrote to ourselves as a reminder that the reprogramming journey will be worth the effort.

It is time to take some more energy boosters as we continue our journey to the Other Side.

There is nothing as affirming as knowing who you are in Christ Jesus. In his book, *Freedom in Christ*, Neil T. Anderson reminds us that we are **accepted, secured, and significant.**

I say "No" to the lie that I am rejected, unloved, or shameful; In Christ, I am accepted. God says:

- I am God's Child (John 1:12);
- I have been redeemed and forgiven of all my sins(Colossians 1:14); and
- I am complete in Christ (Colossians 2:10)

I say "No" to the lie that I am guilty, unprotected, alone, or

abandoned. In Christ, I am secure. God says:

- *I am free from condemnation* (Rom 8:1-2);
- *I cannot be separated from the love of God* (Rom 8:35-39); and
- *I am confident that the good work that God has begun in me will be perfected* (Phillipians 1:6).

I say "No" to the lie that I am worthless, inadequate, helpless, or hopeless. In Christ, I am Significant. God says:

- *I am the salt and the light of the earth* (Matt 5:13-14);
- *I am God's workmanship, created for good works* (Ephesians 3:12); and
- *I can do all things through Christ who strengthens me* (Phillipians 4:13).

LET'S PRAY

Dear heavenly Father, what an awesome opportunity you have granted me to look at my mental maps. I commit myself to be an active co-worker with You in the programming of my mind. I dedicate myself to applying the truth first about what You have to say about a situation. I will learn to say "No" to voices that are not from you. I thank You in advance that I will discover what is Your good, perfect, and accepted will over my life. In Jesus name I pray. Amen

Chapter 4

BUILD MOMENTUM

START SMALL AND FINISH STRONG!

Do not despise these small beginnings, for the Lord rejoices to see the work begin, to see the plumb line in Zerubbabel's hand – Zechariah 4:10 (NLT)

BUILD MOMENTUM

To get to the other side you have to start somewhere. You now know where you are, what is important to you, and where you want to go in challenging some of your mental programming. **It is time for you to get going.** If you are about to do something new, it is advisable to start as small as possible. This is a requirement if you are going to succeed. Starting small will give you the necessary **momentum** and **confidence** to move forward.

This reminds me of a time when I needed to lose weight in preparation for my wedding. I purchased a wedding suite that was two sizes smaller; it was six months before the big day. As a non- runner, I requested help from my brother, who was a reputable long-distance runner to get me into shape to get me to the Other Side. We agreed that I would just join his running schedule during the week for me to get me into shape. What a disaster. I bought brand new running gear to look the part, but that definitely did not help me to be the part. Our running together only lasted for three days with me doing mostly walking and very little running. I started big, which brought more pain and discouragement and not the momentum I needed. We cancelled the arrangement and I started small - walking around the block for a week, picking up the pace the next week, jogging a bit the following week- until I gathered the momentum I wanted. A month before my wedding, I called my brother back, and we started the schedule again.

I am glad to say that I fitted perfectly into my wedding suit on the big day, so don't despise the small beginnings.

So where do you start?

*Suppose one of you wants to build a tower. Won't you **first sit down** and **estimate the cost** to see if you have enough money to complete it? For if you **lay the foundation** and not able to finish it, everyone who sees it will ridicule you. - Luke 14:28-29(NIV)*

You start with a plan. **What** do you want to do? **How** do you want to do it? And **why** do you want to do it? You start with priorities, **first things first**. Where do I start? With what do I start? Who do I need to consult with? Luke reminds us that we need to sit down, plan, and estimate what it will take. Being clear about the costs and timelines, and laying proper foundations will be crucial. There is a popular saying that reminds us that if we **fail to plan,** we are probably **planning to fail.**

Laying proper foundations will allow you to build things instead of wasting your time on wrong priorities. A foundation involves those **basic things** that need to be in **place in order** for you to progress. You need to do some research, speak to people who have done what you are trying to do for you to get an idea of what needs to be in place. In most cases when it comes to the **basics,** there are **no shortcuts**. If you want to become a medical doctor, you cannot skip the basic step of acquiring a medical degree. That basic step applies in the medical profession and in many other areas of your life. **God is also aware of the basics** that need to be in place. He will not compromise on what is required, but He is a Master on "how" it is achieved.

*Similarly, no one who competes as an athlete receives the victor's crown except by **competing according to the rules. The hardworking** farmer should be the first to receive the **share of the crops**. - 2 Timothy 2:5-6 (NIV)*

BUILD MOMENTUM

With anything in life, there are **rules, principles, guidelines, and recipes that make things work**. When you put "handwork" behind these recipes and principles, they normally deliver the crops or the results. Some of these principles are natural and some are spiritual.

Not playing according to these rules will immediately disqualify you from getting to the Other Side.

When you start, there is no time to be fancy. Fanciness comes once you have laid the proper foundations. If you want to bake a chocolate cake, you start with a tried, trusted, and sought after recipe. Once you have mastered the recipe, decorations, and extras can be added to make your cake more distinct from others. As you make this journey to the other side, you have to make up your mind that as rules, principles, guidelines are revealed to you, you will put effort behind them so that you play to win.

Let us see how the above plays out in Daniel's life:

*Then the king ordered Aspenaz, chief of his court officials, to bring into the king's service some of the Israelites from the royal family and nobility - young men **without any physical defect, handsome, showing aptitude** for every kind of learning, **well informed, quick to understand**, and **qualified to serve** in the king's palace. They were to be **trained for three years**, and after that they were to enter the king's service - Daniel 1:3-5 (NIV)*

Daniel was a special person. He was gifted and God had set him apart for His purposes. It is interesting to note that even with everything going for him, he still needed to **complete a three- year training programme to qualify him** to serve in the king's palace. There are certain things that you just have to do to qualify for the Other Side. Quick fixes and shortcuts will not be the order of the day. You will bring your bit, and God will add to it so that you end up at a place better than what you expected.

GETTING TO THE OTHER SIDE

Nothing will help you focus more than having clear and **specific goals to aim for**. While a vision gives you the big picture dream that inspires you, goals give you the specific targets to aim for in pursuit of your vision. A vision also gives you a clear indication that you have arrived at a certain milestone or destination. Probably, more importantly, **goals will shed light** on the things you should **"stop doing"** as they add no real value to what you want to achieve.

Brothers and sisters, I do not consider myself yet to have taken hold of it. But one thing I do: Forgetting what is behind and straining toward what is ahead. ***I press on toward the goal*** *to win the prize for which God has called me heavenward in Christ Jesus - Philippians 3:13-14 (NIV)*

*Therefore, I do not run like someone **running aimlessly**, I do not fight like a boxer beating in the air. No, I strike a **blow to my body** and make it a slave so that after I have preached to others, I myself will **not be disqualified** for the prize - 1 Corinthians 9:27 (NIV)*

A vision without goals will remain just that. It is so important to break your vision up into goals that are **clear, outcome-orientated, time-based, within your influence of contro**l, properly **prioritised**, and small enough to get you going and stretched enough to keep you going. Goals direct your actions and clarity about what you need to achieve will provide enough space and creativity as to how you will do it. Set personal growth goals. The biggest achievement and gratitude that you will experience as you journey to the Other Side will be that the person who started the journey will not be the same person on the Other Side. This will qualify you to enjoy the spoils of getting to the other side.

Let us look at the life of Nehemiah to see the above in motion.

*The king said to me, **"What is it you want?"** Then I prayed to the God of heaven, and I answered the king, "If it pleases the king and*

BUILD MOMENTUM

*if your servant has found favor in his sight, **let him send me** to the city in Judah where my ancestors are buried so **that I can rebuild it.**" Then the king, with the queen sitting beside him, asked me, **"How long will the journey take, and when will you get back**? "It pleased the king to send me; so **I set a time**. I also said to him," If it pleases the king, **may I have** letters to the governors of Trans-Euphrates, so that he will provide me with safe conduct until I arrive in Judah? And **may I have** a letter to Asaph, keeper of the royal park, so that he will give me timber to make beams for the gates of citadel by the temple and for the city wall and for the residence that I will occupy? "And because the gracious **hand of God was on m**e, the **king granted my requests.** - Nehemiah 2:4-8 (NIV)*

It is just amazing to see how **clear and precise** Nehemiah was in his **requests.** His requests were well thought out and well prayed for. God's **favour is put to good use** when we know what we want, why we want it, and how we are going to achieve it. **I sometimes wonder if God is not waiting for us to present to Him what we are waiting on him to do for us.**

Nehemiah had ticked all the boxes, he was clear in his request; it was outcome-orientated and time-based. He was at the heart of the action and he prioritised his actions. In addition, he started small by requesting time away from work to start off before making bigger requests for timber to rebuild the wall. What will you say when someone influential asks you **what you want? What will your response be?** Will it be as detailed and precise as Nehemiah's?

I wonder what would have happened if Nehemiah had spent most of his time and effort to accumulate the timber before asking the king for the go-ahead. He would have wasted his time and resources on the right things, but at the wrong time and in the wrong way. Getting to the place where you understand that there must be priorities is so important in starting your journey to the Other Side. Ask the Lord where you must start.

GETTING TO THE OTHER SIDE

What are the urgent and important things that I need to begin with? What are those things that are easier to do, that will give me the biggest mileage?

*But **seek first** the kingdom of God and his **rightheousness,** and all these **things will be added** to you - Matthew 6:33 (ESV)*

There are certain **things that you seek**, and there are certain **things that will be added** to you; just like Nehemiah who sought the approval and favour of God first. Seeking the right things at the right time in the right way, resulted in all the resources he required to rebuild the wall being added to him. Seeking the wrong things will get you to a place of hard toil. Starting at the wrong place will make you go around in circles, **but how will you know that you started at the right place? Starting at the right place** will create **momentum for you** and things that you worry about will be added, or made available to you, but don't forget, just like Nehemiah, you will be an active participant in all of this. Sometimes the **added stuff** comes in the form of **opportunities and relationships** to which you need to avail yourself.

*Let Pharaoh appoint commissioners over the land to take a **fifth of the harvest** of Egypt during the seven **years of abundance.** They should collect all the food of these good years that are coming and store up the grain **under the authority** of Pharaoh, to be kept in the cities for food. This food should be held in reserve for the country, to be used during the seven years of famine that will come to Egypt, so that the country **may not be ruined** by the famine.*
- Genesis 41:34-36(NIV)

I will provide a quick background to this story. King Pharaoh had a dream and needed someone to interpret it for him. He consulted Joseph who interpreted it. The dream meant that Egypt needed to prepare itself for seven years of famine. It also gave information about what the king needed to do to prepare for it. King Pharaoh

BUILD MOMENTUM

needed Joseph to help him to get to the Other Side of this famine. The counsel Joseph gave Pharaoh was profound for our time as it was for then. **Focus on the right twenty percent of your plenty and it will get you to the Other Side.**

When we cast a vision, we can quickly get excited about all the things that we can do to get going. Sometimes when we are in a moment of crisis, the things we should do to get us out of the situation easily overwhelms us. What we underestimate is that God has put **principles in place and we have a duty to focus on the** most important things in a given situation. Focusing on what is critical produces the rest of the return. This principle has been adopted across the world and has proven to work, for example, twenty percent of any business generates eighty percent of the profits; twenty percent of the staff of an organisation produces eighty percent of an organisation's return. If you can **focus on the right things,** you will be amazed by the **return that you will be able to generate.**

You need to start small and finish strong. As you go, **build** your **confidence, competence, and capacity** to do more and take on more. Confidence that creates momentum will be key for you to handle and adapt to the changes required for you to get to the Other Side.

The Apostle Paul sees it the following way:

> *I have fought the **good fight**, I have **finished the race**, I have **kept the faith** - 2 Timothy 4:7*

Going after a three to **five-year vision** will feel more like a **marathon** than a sprint. Breaking down your vision into **yearly goals will give you a clear direction** and a sense of accomplishment that you need to keep going. Right through this journey, your faith will be tested, and your confidence will be shaken. You will have terrible up runs and smooth down runs. This journey to the other side will give you a good run for your money; it is a good fight as Paul describes it. **Finishing a race qualifies you for the next one.**

Not finishing a race will postpone your progress to the Other Side. The exciting part about finishing a race is all about what you are able to keep that no one can take away from you. **Keeping the faith** your transformative hope, **substance,** and **evidence,** a **deep sense** of **experience** and **education will be some of** your key **takeaways.** The journey to the Other Side is designed to make you a *better* person and not a *bitter* person.

> *My brethren, **count it all joy**, when you fall into various trials, knowing that the **testing of your faith produces** patience, but let patience have its perfect work, that you may be perfect and complete, **lacking nothing** - James 1:3-4 (NKJV)*

Celebrating your external and internal achievements along the way will **keep you going** for the long haul. As you work on and with your vision, don't be surprised by the work the process will do on and in you. **You becoming who you are supposed to be will attract the things that you are supposed to have.** Appreciating the work you have done and the progress you have made will allow the shaping work of faith to continue to do the work in you until you get to a place where you lack nothing. So cheer up, **keep the perspective**, and **enjoy the ride.**

After finishing High School, I had an option to go and work or to go and study. Due to my family background and financial challenges, going to work was by far the best option as I had already secured a job. I considered that it would allow me to earn some much needed income and part-time study opportunities over a longer period. However, in faith I decided to go to university to study full-time.

I enrolled for a teaching degree, which the government funded. I knew that studying full-time would put tremendous strain on me financially to sustain myself during this period. In the middle of my first year, I realised that what I was studying was not for me and studying without another source of income was hard. I changed my field of study to Individual and Organizational Psychology and applied for various bursaries. I was granted a bursary and a part-time job during my study, and the rest is history. I finished my first degree within the three-year period, fully paid for by the bursary scheme. I had a part-time job over weekends and holidays, which sorted out the rest.

This sacrifice put the foundations in place for future studies that took me to some of the best universities in the world, and a career that took me to the highest level in my field. The three-year vision fundamentally changed the trajectory of my life.

"GETTING YOU TO THE OTHER SIDE"
GROWTH PLAN

Build Momentum Mastery

LET'S PRAY

Dear Heavenly Father what an exciting time for me to get going with what You have entrusted me with. Show me today where I need to start, the things I need to seek first so that You can add to them. Show me Your ways, Your rules, Your principles, Your guidelines, and Your recipes that I need to follow. I accept that whatever You are going to do will be done with me and through me.
In Jesus name, Amen.

GETTING TO THE OTHER SIDE

Let's get practical:

Read through the three-year vision letter that you wrote to yourself in chapter 2. Prayerfully decide which areas of your life you need to focus on. These areas will make the biggest contribution to your vision. This might include areas like your family, finances, education, or your career. You should try to narrow it down to a maximum of three areas. Below you will find an example of how you can unpack your life area into goals with corresponding actions.

Area of my life	Where do I start in Year 1?	How does Year 2 look like?	Where would I like to be at the end of Year 3 "The other side"
For example: Family	1. Praying about the future of my kids and seeking God's guidance. 2. Having a conversation with my wife to hear what is in her heart for our kids. 3. Having a conversation with my kids to hear what is in their hearts. 4. Starting to look at options, routines and resources required for…?	1. Manage and steward the financial plan to secure university fees. 2. Apply for bursaries and secure places at universities etc. 3. Have	I am a role model father to my kids, helping them to navigate and transition into young adulthood.

Goal for Year One: To have a financial and transition plan in place in preparation for my daughter's going to university by the end of October this year.

BUILD MOMENTUM

What will be the top three things that will help to achieve this goal?
1. Having a conversation once a week with the family until we complete and agree on a plan.
1. Having a grip and understanding of our financial situation and the cost implications of universities and additional costs.
2. Having different options as to how this can work.

Goal for Year Two: Follow through on the financial and transition plan and make adjustments where necessary by November this year.

Now it is time for you to unpack your chosen life areas:

1. Select your life area that will make the biggest contribution for you to achieve your three to five year vision.
3. Describe where you would like to be by the end of Year Three.
4. Where would you like to start (Year One)? Remember to start small so that you can build momentum.
5. Once you know where you want to start, set a goal for yourself. Remember you need to set some smart goals. They must be clear, precise, time-bound and must be within your control.
6. Once you have set a goal for yourself, think of actions that will contribute to the achievement of that goal.
7. It is time for you to get going and do not forget to celebrate your achievements along the way.

Let us take some more energy boosters for the journey ahead:

2 Chronicles 15:7(NIV) - But as for you, be strong, and do not give up, for your work will be rewarded.

James 2:17 (NKJV) - Thus also faith by itself, if it does not have works, is dead.

Proverbs 21:5 (NIV) - The plans of the diligent lead to profit as surely as haste leads to poverty.

GETTING TO THE OTHER SIDE

Proverbs 3:6 (NKJV) - In all your ways acknowledge Him, And He will direct your paths.

LET'S PRAY

Dear heavenly Father, I commit my plans to you. These goals that I have set have put my faith into motion. I am excited for the days ahead. Continue to guide and support me on this journey. In Jesus name, Amen.

Chapter 5

PACK LIGHT

LETTING GO OF THE HOLD THAT OTHERS HAVE ON YOU

Then Peter came to Him and said, "Lord how often shall my brother sin against me, and I forgive him? Up to seven times? Jesus said to him, "I do not say to you, up to seven times, but up to seventy times seven. - Matthew 18:21-22(NKJV)

Getting to the Other Side feels more like a five-day **survival hike** through a bushy and mountainous terrain than a fancy trip to an exotic destination. Packing light and packing the right things will be vital to your survival. Nothing will increase the **weight of your bag like unforgiveness.**

Unforgiveness with its fruits of bitterness and anger are poison to your soul. It will **cloud your thinking, decision-making** and drain your **emotional energy.** Jesus knew that and requested his disciples to forgive as often as they could; however, this is much easier said than done. Jesus does not at all refer to the perpetrator during this exchange, because **forgiveness** is all about your **well-being as the victim.** Unforgiveness replays the impact of the traumatic event repeatedly while destroying you. In most cases, the perpetrator is unaware that they have wronged you and remains unaffected. The need for vengeance plays out in anger and bitterness that just fuels and prolongs the pain. With all the above going on, **forgiveness** will seldomly occur naturally, but needs to be made through a **deliberate choice.** The reality of unforgiveness is that some of the people that we need to forgive have passed on and we are still carrying the heavy bag of bitterness and anger. Choosing to **forgive** will start the **healing process.**

GETTING TO THE OTHER SIDE

> *Jesus said, "Father forgive them, for they do not know what they are doing. "And they divided up his clothes by casting lots"*
> *- Luke 23:34 (NIV)*

This is the greatest forgiveness story of all time and a reminder that **bad things** can happen to **good people.** There is a difference between forgiving the person and forgiving the deed. **Forgiveness** does **not excuse** or make the deed right. It acknowledges the deed with its corresponding consequences that in certain times can be overcome or sometimes you just have to live with it. Forgiving the person will determine how well you will be able to **live with or overcome the consequences.**

When I was six years old, my brother shot me with a slingshot in a freak accident. My right eye was injured. I landed up in hospital for two weeks, bitter and angry with him. Today I am half-blind in my right eye, which impacts my twenty-twenty vision. This has impaired my physical appearance; the right eye is slightly smaller, and it has prevented me from playing certain sports. I forgave my brother not long after the incident, and I am gladly living with the consequences. Our relationship today is still very close and I love him to bits.

> *For I will **forgive their wickedness** and will **remember their sins no more** - Hebrews 8:12 (NIV)*

Forgiveness does not require you to forget. What needs to be **erased** from your memory, through the healing process of forgiveness, is the **painful consequence** of anger and bitterness. I cannot forget what happened to me when I was six-years old, but when I think about it, it does not stir up feelings of anger, bitterness, or vengeance. **God cannot forget; He is all knowing.** When He forgives us, **He decides not to bring up our past** to belittle us, but He has truly forgiven us so that we can heal and learn from our past and continue to move forward.

> *For if you forgive other people when they sin against you, your heavenly Father will also forgive you. - Matthew 6:14 (NIV)*

Forgiveness is very much a **"pay it forward" act**. Not forgiving others indicates a lack of appreciation of how much forgiveness **you and I might need** for our journey to the Other Side.
So let's face it, we don't get things right all the time, and in some cases **we contribute to the pain** and harm of others. The reality of the matter is that you cannot get what you are not willing to give.
Why is this so important? Bitterness and anger towards others **will block you from receiving** or experiencing God's forgiveness. It is not that God does not want to forgive you; it is that **you will be unable to receive it**. The main person in forgiveness is you; the main beneficiary of forgiveness is you.

> *And "don't sin be letting anger control you," Don't let the sun go down while you are still angry, for anger gives a foothold to the devil. - Ephesians 4:27*

Unforgiveness is the prime cause of anger and bitterness; it **opens the door for the devil to influence** and control your life. We can all agree that anger and bitterness are dark and lonely places. When you forgive, you are not only kick-starting the healing process, but you also release any foothold that the devil might have on you. Forgiveness is not an easy choice to make, but it is definitely a wise one.

Now that you know the importance of forgiveness, **make it easier for others to do so too**. Make their journey a bit lighter as you journey along.

> *Therefore, if you are offering your gift at the altar and there remember that your brother or sister has something against you, leave your gift in front of the altar. First go and be reconciled to them; then come and offer your gift. - Matthew 5:24(NIV)*

What happens to the perpetrator?

Repay no one evil for evil. Have regard for good things in the sight of all men. If it is possible, as much as it depends on you, live peaceably with all men. Beloved, do not avenge yourselves; but rather give place to wrath; for it is written, "Vengeance is Mine, I will repay," says the Lord. - Romans 12;17-19 (NKJV)

The most important part is to **set good and healthy boundaries** between you and the perpetrator; it depends on you. **Forgiveness is not agreeing that** the "act" was right or allowing that someone repeats it, but it is about setting wise boundaries so that you can live in peace with one another. This will allow God to take care of the situation on your behalf, to bring about reconciliation where necessary, healing and letting go or repayment. Trust God during this process. He will know best. **Forgiveness** in most cases is the **beginning of the healing process**. Be patient with yourself, once you kick-start the process, God will do the rest.

Unforgiveness is not the only act that will cause you to carry **unwanted extra weight** on your journey to the Other Side. The unrealistic expectations you allow others to place on you, and the **unrealistic expectations** you place on others can also become a **heavy burden to carry.**

The burden of unrealistic expectations

*Now a certain man was there who had an **infirmity thirty-eight years**. When Jesus saw him lying there, and knew that he had already **been in that condition a long time**, He said to him, "Do you want to be made well?" The sick man answered Him, "Sir, I **have no man to put me into the pool** when the water is stirred up; but while I am coming, another steps down before me." Jesus said to him, "Rise, take up your bed and walk." And immediately the man was made well, took up his bed, and walked.*
- John 5:5-8 (NKJV)

On our journey to the Other Side, **we need to distinguish between Godly goals and our own human desires** we have for other people in our circle of influence. Just like the lame man at the pool, we often plan our journey to the Other Side with other people in mind playing along or doing their part. This delays our journey, in the case of the lame man it was thirty-eight years. The amount of **unnecessary frustration** and burden to try to **convince and change other people** to play along can be a waste of your energy. We often use phrases like: "I will become a better husband if only my wife can…." , "I will become a better father if only …" "I will be healed if only someone can put me into the pool". This happened to the lame man for thirty-eight years. By doing this, we are delaying our own journey and we are carrying the burden of someone else's change.

If you set Godly goals that **are within your control,** and commit them to God so that He can become a co-worker with you, it **will go a long way** to getting you **to your Other Side**. Praying for people around you should be the only expectation that you should place on yourself. The inability of certain people you depend on to meet certain expectations should not prevent you from moving forward. You will be surprised to see how much support you will get from unexpected places when you decide to move forward with only you and God. It is time for you to **let go of the unrealistic expectations** that you have placed on others. Becoming who you need to be will be the greatest contribution that you will make to others.

The book of Samuel lets us into another amazing story that describes the limitations that the expectations of others can put on us:

*Saul replied, "**You are not able to go** out against this Philistine and fight him; **you are only** a young man, and he has been a warrior from his youth." But David said to Saul, "Your servant has been keeping his father's sheep. When a lion or a bear came and carried off a sheep from the flock, I went after it, struck it, and rescued the sheep from its mouth. When it turned on me, I seized it by its hair,* *struck it, and killed it. Your servant has killed both the lion and the bear; this uncircumcised Philistine will be like one of them, because he has defied the armies of the living God. The Lord who rescued me from the paw of the lion and the paw of the bear will rescue me from the hand of this Philistine." Saul said to David, "Go, and the Lord will be with you." Then* **Saul dressed David in his own tunic***. He put a coat of armor on him and a bronze helmet on his head. David fastened on his sword over the tunic and tried walking around, because* **he was not used to them. "I cannot go in these,"** *he said to Saul, "because I am not used to them." So* **he took them off.** *- 1 Samuel 17:32-39 (NIV)*

People can easily **put you into a box** based on their perceptions or assumptions about you. In most cases, people look at you through their own limitations. People use criteria based on race, gender, age, education, background, experience, upbringing, social and financial status, and many more criteria to judge you. The lens they use to judge may either support or limit you. In David's case, his age and lack of military training became the defining and limiting criteria. When **people** start to **think less of you** they are inclined to **place** their **unrealistic expectations** on you with the hope that it will help you, but in essence it stifles you. King Saul at this time was an old man not ready to face Goliath, but he was quick to impose the way he would have done it on David. Dressing David up in his armour made him look the part, in the eyes of Saul and others, but he could not be the part. David admits that he could not get to the Other Side dressed in Saul's armour; he just could not move. The **unrealistic expectations** of others can **stifle you** to a place where you just **cannot move.**

It is so important to **own your stories, your background and your experiences** that have made you who you are and that have brought you to where you are. David went through public schooling; the lion and the bear experiences while looking after his father's sheep. While he was receiving his training, Saul was attending private schooling, military school; both of them were preparing for kingship. It is quite ironic that David made a far better King than Saul. **Confidence comes** when we can **embrace where we come from** when we slay giants along the way to our Other Side. I am curious to know whose armour you are wearing. Is it your parents', your religion, your culture, your partner's, your race or gender grouping, your colleagues, your peer group, or your boss'? Just like David, it is time for you to re-evaluate your armour and **take off what prevents you from being your authentic self.**

We have to pack light if we are going to make it to the other side. In this chapter, we highlighted the heaviness and burden of **unforgiveness, the expectations we place on others, and the unrealistic expectations** we allow others to place on us. It is our responsibility to pack light and keep our travelling bag as light as possible as we journey to the other side. Keep on forgiving, keep on being the best version of yourself, and keep on shutting your heart to the limiting expectations of others.

"GETTING YOU TO THE OTHER SIDE"
GROWTH PLAN
Pack Light Mastery

LET'S PRAY

Dear heavenly Father, I want to thank you for making it possible for me to forgive those that have harmed me. Bring to my remembrance the people that I need to forgive during this time. I choose today to forgive. Forgiveness is good for me and it allows me to heal. I am glad that vengeance belongs to you. Help me to set healthy boundaries so that I can live in peace with others. I commit myself to setting goals that are authentically mine; within my own control; goals that require Your help to achieve. Continue to help me to protect my heart from the criticism and unrealistic expectations of others. In Jesus name I pray, Amen

Let's get practical:

1. Think about a person or an event that requires your forgiveness.
1. Think about what he or she did, or failed to do
2. Share the painful feelings that you have experienced. What was the feeling?
3. What have been the consequences of their actions.
4. Appreciate that despite whatever has happened to you, you are still here and God has granted you the opportunity to forgive so that you can lighten your bag as you journey to the Other Side.

Let us do the Prayer of Forgiveness:

Lord Jesus I choose to forgive….. (name of the person), for… (What he or she failed to do) because it made me feel….(share the painful feelings). I choose not to hold on to my resentment and anger, I let go of my right to make things right in my own way, and I ask you to heal me from my damaged emotions. Thank you for setting me free from the bondage of unforgiveness and bitterness. I choose to live with the tangible consequences of the act, but not with the painful emotions. I ask that you bless those that have hurt me, and that You do what needs to be done for restoration. In Jesus name, Amen

Do the above for every person that you need to forgive in this season.

Lifting the burden of unrealistic expectations

Identify areas in your life where you find it difficult to move. Identify the limiting expectations that you have placed on others or that others have placed on you. Renounce those expectations and start setting goals that are within your control and that you and God can work on.

Let us take some healing boosters for our journey ahead:

I am convinced and confident of this very thing that He who has begun a good work in you will (continue to) perfect and complete it until the day of Christ Jesus - Philippians 1:6 (AMP)
Now to him who is able to do immeasurably more than all we ask or imagine, according to his power that is at work within us - Ephesians 3:20 (NIV)

If we confess our sins, he is faithful and just and will forgive us our sins and purify us from all unrighteousness - 1 John 1:9 (NIV)

GETTING TO THE OTHER SIDE

For my thoughts are not your thoughts, neither are your ways my ways, declares the Lord. As the heavens are higher than the earth, so are my ways higher than your ways and my thoughts than your thoughts. - Isaiah 55: 8-9(NIV)

LET'S PRAY

Dear Heavenly Father. Thank you for making my bag lighter as I journey to the Other Side. Burdens were lifted and yokes were destroyed. Guard my heart and my mind. Flood my heart with peace and an assurance that You are in control. In Jesus name, Amen.

Chapter 6

PAYING YOUR OWN WAY

YOUR ROLE AS A STEWARD

"Whoever can be trusted with very little can also be trusted with much, and whoever is dishonest with very little will also be dishonest with much." - Luke 16:10 (NIV)

PAYING YOUR OWN WAY

There is nothing in life that **will increase what you need** in the future as being a **good steward** of what you already have. The Other Side is a better place than where you started. It is a place of more - a journey of increase. To be able to do so you would need to have an **ownership mindset and a stewardship heart** that God can trust. Being a good steward with the little that you have will automatically result in you being entrusted with more. At the heart of stewardship sits the fundamental belief that **not everything that you own is yours**, but it has been entrusted to you to **look after** in such a way that it **produces more.**

As we picked up in the previous chapters, just as favor starts with God,(flows to you and then to others) so will accountability for what you have been entrusted with. **God has this earnest desire to keep you accountable** for what He has entrusted to you, not to judge or condemn you, but with the desire to want to entrust you with more. **Dishonesty** occurs when you **diminish the value** of what you have **been entrusted with** by neglecting things that are within your control. Your stewardship should be a fair reflection of your desperation to get to the Other Side.

How is your family, your finances, your health, your marriage, your parenting, your education, your calling, your purpose, and your possessions? What will happen if God calls you today to give an account of what He has entrusted you with?

Most of us **suffer** from an **ownership heart** and a **stewardship mindset.** We own everything we have so we do not need to give an account to anyone but ourselves. This type of mindset drives a **false sense of confidence** that places an unnecessary burden on you to make everything happen in your life. If it is going to be, it is going to be up to me. You will even go so far as to lie to yourself and to others to get you where you need to be. You will soon get to the place where the entrustment of God stops over your life and you have to **work hard for everything** you need in life.

Stewardship is one of the most important keys that you would need to unlock your way to the Other Side. Disregard this principle at your own peril.

I remember in my early thirties when we went through financial difficulties and almost lost everything we had. It was an embarrassing time in my life, but also the most educational. The period just before this, we were doing well for ourselves and people admired us for being a prosperous and blessed young couple. As we consolidated our finances to plan the way forward, I decided to purchase two new vehicles to give people out there an impression that we were still doing well. Eventually, we could not afford the payments but new jobs became available just in time for us to keep the vehicles and move forward. It was not long before these vehicles started to give us problems and we traded them in for new ones. We paid back a lot of money to settle the vehicles and it was painful. God spoke to me during that time, reminding me that it was not His plan to entrust me with these vehicles, but mine, and because of my dishonesty towards other people, I was suffering a financial loss. What God wanted to teach me was to be faithful with the little, but I had other plans in mind.

In most cases when the Bible speaks about stewardship, it talks about money. Our relationship with money indicates the heart of stewardship that we sit with.

> *A feast is made for laughter, and wine makes the life glad: and money is the answer for all things - Ecclesiastes 10:19 (WEB)*

Money plays such an important part in our lives. If you reflect back to the letter that you wrote to yourself in Chapter Two, you should not be surprised about the **importance money will play** to get you to the other side. Money will be the answer to quite a few things to get you to the Other Side or to make the journey a bit easier. Money will never make you happy, but the lack thereof will make you unhappy. You should not be running after money, but **through good stewardship find a way for money to run after you**. You should not use money as a proxy to the quality of your stewardship. If you are not disciplined in how you steward your money, it will be a good indicator of how you steward other areas of your life. **Your future vision will need provision and stewardship will be at the heart of making it possible.**

> *So if you have not been trustworthy in handling worldly wealth, who will trust you with true riches? And if you have not been trustworthy with someone else's property, who will give you property of your own - Luke 16:11 (NIV)*

You must start changing your mindset. **Everything that you own today has been entrusted to you**. Some things that you are part of belong to someone else that you have the privilege of being a part of.

How well you look after the above will determine the next level of your entrustment. **True riches** speak about acquiring the required **wisdom for you to navigate** your life's journey to the other side.

GETTING TO THE OTHER SIDE

> *That night God appeared to Solomon and said to him, "Ask whatever you want me to give to you."* **Give me wisdom and knowledge,** *that I may lead this people, for who is able to govern this great people of yours?' God said to Solomon, "Since this is* **your heart's desire** *and you have not asked for wealth, possessions or honor, nor for the death of your enemies, and since you have not asked for long life but for wisdom and knowledge to govern my people over whom I have made you king, therefore wisdom and knowledge will be given to you.* **And I will also give you** *wealth, possession and honor, such as no king who was before you ever had and none after will have.*
> - 2 Chronicles 1:8,10-12 (NIV)

Solomon reminds us that **stewardship is a heart condition** and you realize **true riches when God grants wisdom (know how).** Understanding what God has entrusted to you and seeing it as a privilege and a great responsibility will make you push aside your own ambitions. In addition, it will sometimes help you to ignore your selfish desires in pursuit of **something greater that you need to give an account for. Stewardship produces wisdom and wisdom produces everything else.**

Luke also reminds us that we should be mindful of what we become a part of. It is sad to see how people **treat other people's possessions** not knowing that taking care of those belongings is a test to see if they **can be trusted with their own.** Mismanagement of other people's possessions takes away and robs them of progress and robs them of their future ownership, therefore, you have to be selective in what you become a part of. **Taking from others is not the same as being entrusted with your own.** While both will feel like something has been added to your life, one is daylight robbery through dishonesty and the other is genuine entrustment that will get you to the Other Side. If you are part of something where you cannot be trusted with someone else's property, cannot exercise a heart of stewardship and a mindset of ownership, and you are there with a selfish agenda, it is time for you to walk away from it, because you will do more harm than good.

Quite a few years ago, as an executive, I was working for a human resources director of one of the big banks. He is someone I respected but not always agreed with. As I started to complain about this, God reminded me that my boss was entrusted with a certain mandate from the organization and that I had the privilege to be part of it. God called me to stewardship of what was not mine. The director's mandate was in someone else's possession. With a change of heart, I walked into my boss' office and promised him that I would work with him to the best of my ability. The measure of my stewardship would be when I saw him succeed. This commitment lasted for three years. During that time, my life changed drastically, many opportunities opened for me to grow locally and internationally; I got promoted, experienced significant financial increase, built meaningful friendships, led great projects that helped to change the trajectory of the organization, all under the direction of my boss. During that time, he received accolades and recognition for the work we did. He even won the National Human Resources Director Award. Today we are great friends. It pays to be a steward, especially when you have to take care of someone else's possessions.

The above experience captures one of the most defining moments in my career. This experience has changed the trajectory of my life for good. It helped me to make progress in many ways, and helped to get me to the other side. This reminds me of this amazing scripture:

Whatever you do, work at it with all your heart, as working for the Lord, not for human masters, since you know that you will receive an inheritance from the Lord as a reward. It is the Lord that you are serving - Colossians 3:23-24(NIV)

So how will you know that you can be trusted?

GETTING TO THE OTHER SIDE

When your **heart is in something,** you need **very little motivation** to make the necessary sacrifices to succeed. In most cases, these sacrifices precede the reward, but you will be doing it in service to others, knowing that you are investing into your future. One thing is for sure: you will have to give your way to the Other Side. **Giving yourself wholeheartedly in service** to your purpose and vision for your life will make you transcend the transactional arrangement of work and reward that you receive from mere men, but **you will be entrusted with an inheritance** that comes from God. **You will have to be the biggest investor into your own vision.** Wholeheartedness does not come cheap. **There is a big difference between receiving a transactional reward for work done and an inheritance.** Inheritance feels more like receiving what is already yours and stewardship is the key that unlocks it. Whatever desires you may have to make things better around you, God sits with the same desires, but you are going to have to trust Him by **standing in service to others, so that He can entrust you.**

You have to start seeing yourself as an appointed steward over your vision. It is not yours; God is trusting you with it to accomplish a certain change in your lifetime. You must treat it as your own, manage it as your own, knowing that you have to give an account for it that comes from a steward's heart.

> "Bring the whole tithe into the storehouse, that there may be food in my house. Test me in this," says the Lord Almighty, "And see if I will not throw open the floodgates of heaven and pour out so much blessing that there will not be enough room to store it.
> - Malachi 3:10 (NIV)

As a steward, you can access your inheritance (blessing) **deciding to become part of God's economic system.** God's only way to tangibly bless others is through others. There is no bigger way to show God that you trust Him than giving to this system. However, you need to be clear about what you will give: a tithe; where you will

PAYING YOUR OWN WAY

give - the storehouse and why you will give - so there may be food in my house. On your way to the Other Side look around you and decide **how you can become part of someone else's miracle, someone else's blessing.** Do not give under compulsion or obligation. Be intentional, sow into an environment where your seed will make a difference.

While building relationships will always be reciprocal in nature for it to be viable, this type of giving is over and above asking you to give slightly more than what you get in return. This giving allows you to become part of God's work here on earth. It gives God no option but to fill your storehouse with more stuff to give and to **thank you for being part of His work here on earth.**

There is a time when I went through a financial crisis. I only had R2500 ($150) left in my bank account with quite a few creditors demanding payments. I woke up one morning with a heavy heart; my financial woes overwhelmed me. When I spoke to God about it, the only words I could hear were: "Do you trust Me?" While I was watching a Christian Television network, a certain ministry was making a request for financial support; to be part of God's work here on earth, I was convicted to sow a seed in support. The seed was R2500. Doing this was not easy as it was my very last, but the words "Do you trust me?" kept ringing in my ears.

A few days later, I got an unexpected call from my previous employer offering me a job that I had not even applied for. That was not all. They even asked me how much money I wanted to be paid. This was the end of my financial woes and a few years later, I claimed a debt free status.

A heart of giving is at the heart of you being a good steward. You and I are going to need ample blessings to get us to the Other Side. It is not about what you give, but if you have a heart to give. Do you want to be an intentional vehicle through which God can be a blessing to others? Money is a good proxy of our stewardship, but of course our stewardship is more than just money. Your time, your gifts and talents, your purpose and calling, your possessions, and your relationships that you place in service towards others count as stewardship too.

> *Now he who supplies seed to the sower and bread for food will also supply and increase your store of seed and will enlarge the harvest of your righteousness. You will be enriched in every way so that you can be generous on every occasion and through us and your generosity will result in thanksgiving to God. This service that you perform is not only supplying the needs of the Lord's people but is also overflowing in many expressions of thanks to God - 2 Corinthians 9:10-12 (NIV)*

If you have a **heart of a sower** then God will supply a seed so that you can be generous in every occasion. You are going to have to pay forward what you want to see happening in your own life. If you are going sow for it, **you don't have to fight for it.**

When we started our own ministry, it was not long before the building that we were in became too small and God started to speak to us about trusting Him for a bigger one. One morning on my way to work, one of our local Christian radio stations was raising funds for a new building. As I listened to the request, I was convicted to sow into the project on behalf of our Church for the new building that we were trusting God for. God laid a certain amount on my heart and I called in to make a pledge. What dawned on me after doing so was that we might not even have this amount of money in the Church account. On my arrival at work, the treasurer of the church phoned me to let me know that someone had made a huge deposit into our Church account that same morning. I was not surprised that is was the same amount that I pledged. Three months later, God blessed us with our new building that we paid for in cash through His generosity.

A giving and generous heart for God to do something through your life activates the stewardship blessing. God does not take lightly that you are positioning yourself to become part of His miracles in other people's lives. Just be intentional and be ready to give an account of why you give, what you give, and if your giving has accomplished the outcome. Giving is a way to show God that you trust Him. **The more you trust Him, the more He entrusts you.**

Remember this: Whoever sows sparingly will also reap sparingly, and whoever sows generously will also reap generously. Each of you should give what you have decided in your heart to give, not reluctantly or under compulsion, for God loves a cheerful giver. And God is able to bless you abundantly, so that in all things at all times, having all that you need, you will abound in every good work.
- 2 Corinthians 9:6-8(NIV)

Stewardship is a heart condition, your place of Godly conviction and authenticity. Being part of God's miracles in the lives of others starts with a conviction in your heart. It is a conviction that you need to obey. It does not come through manipulation that plays on your emotions or sympathies, or feeding the failures or habits of a dishonest request. **There is purpose behind stewardship, sowing of seed into good ground, expecting a return that God will orchestrate through various channels coming from only one Source who is Him.**

Quite a few years ago, my wife spoke to me about leaving her corporate job to pursue full time ministry and entrepreneurial businesses in the field of Early Childhood Development (ECD). I could immediately sense that this was close to her heart and something that God spoke to her about. She had a successful corporate career at the time and her income to our household made a significant contribution to our standard of living. We needed to act as good stewards to this call over her life and we immediately made plans for her to resign and for us to re-adjust our lifestyle, as this would be a zero paying venture for quite some time. While following through on this commitment a new job opportunity opened up at my workplace and I applied for it. After attending the interview, I was convinced that I would not qualify for the job. To my surprise, I did get the job and the salary increase they had offered me was exactly the amount of money my wife earned. This allowed my wife to cheerfully devote herself to being a blessing in the ECD space, helping God to do His work in the lives of children and parents in the communities that we serve. Today she is also a proud owner of a few thriving ECD businesses.

You are going to have to give of yourself if you are going to get to your Other Side. As mentioned before, having a steward's heart is half of the story, but it should also be buttressed by an ownership mindset. This ownership mindset will determine how well you will manage what you have been entrusted with. How well do you plan, organize, and control what you have been entrusted with so that it produces more? **The stewardship heart infuses what you do with the essence of giving and service, while the ownership mindset makes you take care of someone else's possessions as if they were your own and your destiny depends on it.**

> *Again, it will be like a man going on a journey, who called his servants and entrusted his wealth to them. To one he gave five bags of gold, to another two bags, and to another one bag, each according to his ability. Then he went on his journey. The man who had received five bags of gold went at once and put his money to work and gained five bags more. - Matthew 25:14-16 (NIV)*

Putting what God has entrusted you to work so that it can produce the desired outcome, will make you experience increase as you journey to the Other Side. **God will not entrust you with more than you can handle; it will always be according to your ability.** Interesting enough, through the process of stewardship, you increase what has been entrusted to you and by default, you increase your ability, because the measure of your ability goes together with the measure of your entrustment. **Good stewardship grows your internal value.**

PAYING YOUR OWN WAY

The Lord has blessed me with two beautiful daughters. I would admit that I had no idea how to be a father - never mind a good father, when all of this started. All I knew was that I was entrusted to be one. My role as dad is to take care of my daughters in such a way that it brings the best out of them. This means that I need to be open to learning and growing with them so that I can become the father that I need to be. Being an ideal father will help them to become the women that they need to be. Having a steward heart and an ownership mindset on my parenting has helped me to grow and develop. It is daunting to say the least; it involves not always getting it right and unlearning the unhealthy mental models of parenting which I was exposed to. I receive regular feedback from my daughters and my wife, and mentoring from experts in the field through their books and seminars. The feedback from my family and mentoring teaches me what I can do to improve as a parent and knowing that I am ultimately accountable to God, who has been the greatest adviser of them all, who gave me them in the first place. Parenting has significantly changed my life and it will continue to do so as I continue to commit myself to stewardship.

The more you apply the principle of stewardship to areas of your life, the more productive your life will be. Take care of your health, wealth, time, gifts and talents, relationships, family, marriage, and your mandated assignment here on earth in such a way that you grow what you have and at the same time grow who you are.

"GETTING YOU TO THE OTHER SIDE"
GROWTH PLAN
Paying Your Own Way Mastery

LET'S PRAY

Dear heavenly father, thank You for entrusting me with much in my life. I commit myself to giving an account to You. Forgive me in areas of my life where I have not been a good steward. Cultivate within me a steward's heart with an ownership mindset. I believe that stewardship will unlock the true inheritance that you have in store for me. Holy Spirit show me how I should improve my stewardship in all areas of my life. In Jesus Name I pray. Amen.

Let's get practical.

Tighten up your Stewardship

1. Review your **"Let's get practical"** section in Chapter 4.
2. Review your commitments and see how you can improve your stewardship.
3. Take a deep look at your relationship with your finances. Make commitments and follow through to handle your money God's way. If you are part of a local Church, commit to being more faithful in giving your tithes and offerings.
4. Look at areas of your life where you are working for someone else. Change your mind and heart towards them. Commit to becoming a great steward of what they have entrusted you with.
5. Visualize being a great steward in all areas of your life and

write the following note to yourself; "I see myself being a great steward when …"
6. Commit this note to the Lord in prayer.

Let's take some nutrients to build us up into great stewards.

Commit your works to the LORD, and your thoughts will be established. - Proverbs 16:3 (NIV)

Wealth gained hastily will dwindle, but whoever gathers little by little will increase it - Proverbs 13:11(ESV)

You shall remember the Lord your God, for it is he who gives you power to get wealth, that he may confirm his covenant that he swore to your fathers, as it is this day. - Deuteronomy 8:18(ESV)

His master said to him, "Well done, good and faithful servant, you have been faithful over a little; I will set you over much. Enter into the joy of the Master" - Matthew 25:21 (ESV)

But seek first the kingdom of God and his righteousness, and all these things will be added to you - Matthew 6:33 (ESV)

LET'S PRAY

Great stewardship is my portion in Jesus Name Amen.

Chapter 7
DETOUR
WHEN THINGS GO WRONG!

And we know that in all things God works for the good for those who love him, who have been called according to his purpose - Romans 8:28 (NIV)

DETOUR

It is a given that **things will not work out exactly** the way you have planned your journey to get to the Other Side. Unexpected things and sometimes life changing events will derail you or even take you on a major detour. When the Bible states that "**all things will work together**" for your good, it literally means **all** things. Not just the good things, not just the bad things, not just the expected things, **but also all things will somehow work** together for your good.

This passage always reminds me of a chocolate cake recipe. Some of the **ingredients** needed to make a chocolate cake **do not taste good individually,** while others do. It is only when these ingredients are **mixed together** that they produce a **tasty chocolate cake.**

Where you are going, you will need a **variety of ingredients** from different places to get you to your Other Side. Some of these **ingredients will come from good** times in your life and some of them will **come from really dark and lonely places**. For these ingredients to work, you would need to stay connected to the love of God over your life. You have to allow Him to show you how all of these are connected to your purpose and your calling here on earth. Many things will not make sense when we go through them, but it is amazing how these **things start to make sense when we look back** over our lives. As some would say, hindsight is a perfect science. Shaping your character in preparation for God to entrust you with much sometimes requires a major detour.

The book of Romans also reminds us that God's major concern is for you to live out the purpose for which He called you; the "why" and the "what" of your life. The "how" you will get there will always be open for debate and re-route. When you **become fixated on the "how", your detour might just end up in a dead end**.

There is an amazing story in the Bible about Joseph and his brothers, and how things went terribly wrong for him. This is what he thought.

Jacob loved Joseph more than any of his other children because Joseph had been born to him in his old age. So one day Jacob had a special gift made for Joseph - a beautiful robe
- Genesis 37:3 (NLT)

This caused so much trouble between Jacob's sons that Joseph's brothers became so envious of him that they wanted to kill him. What made matters worse was that not only did Jacob think Joseph was special, but even God had a special assignment for Joseph that He revealed to him in a dream. In his innocence, he shared the dreams that foretold that his brothers and father would bow down to him one day. This infuriated the family and made Joseph's brothers even more determined to kill him.

Where Joseph was standing, he was destined for greatness, set apart by his father and earmarked by God. His journey to the other side was guaranteed and paved with roses. When we have everything going for us, it is so easy to forget that God may have other plans to get us to the Other Side. If we continue to follow the life of Joseph, his brothers threw him into a pit, stripped him of his robe, and decided not to kill him but sell him as a slave. They went home and told their father that a wild animal had killed him. He ended up in one of Pharaoh's prisons and eventually interpreted some of Pharaoh's dreams that helped him save his kingdom. Eventually, Pharaoh appointed Joseph as Governor over his land.

What a detour! He went from his place to the pit; from the pit to the prison; and from the prison to the palace. I wonder if Joseph would have been so outspoken if he knew that this was going to be his journey to the Other Side. **He understandably felt disappointed, rejected, and betrayed by his family after all the near death experiences that he faced in the pit, the prison and even in the palace**.

Joseph said to his brothers, "Come near to me. "So they came near. He said, "I am your brother Joseph, whom you sold into Egypt. But do not be troubled or angry with yourselves because you sold me here. For God sent me before you to save your life. For the land has been without food these two years. And there are five more years without ploughing or gathering. God sent me before you to make sure that your people will keep living on the earth. Now many of you will be saved. - Genesis 45:4-7 (NLV)

Part of Joseph being set up in this way was God's way to ensure that he ended up in the palace so that he could be instrumental in saving the lives of his family during the time of a seven year famine. He pardoned his brothers and reminded them that if it was not for them, selling him into Egypt, that all of this would not have been possible. **All things do work out for your good!**

In the early stages of ministry, my wife and I sacrificed everything we had to build a church in the local community where we come from. Life was tough but exciting at the same time. My immediate family was part of the origins of the ministry. We were all new to this and we had a lot to learn. Everyone had a role to play and we did so with great dedication and sacrifice, which gave us hope for the future. It came as a surprise when the entire extended family decided to resign from the church citing personal reasons that were mostly directed at me.

GETTING TO THE OTHER SIDE

This left my wife and I all alone to steer the ship, and at the time the task just seemed overwhelming. They left us for dead. I questioned God's purpose and calling over our lives and I was willing just to shut everything down and move on. During that tough time, we decided to take a break and we went away for a weekend. While I was in the pool having fun with my daughter, a stranger walked up to me and said to me that God told him to tell me not to give up on ministry, and that God will carry us through all the hardships. I could not believe what I was hearing from a total stranger. We went back to church and invested even more of our time and money into the ministry. We did all the work and we were everywhere. Monday to Monday, we sacrificed. Those were some of the best years in the ministry when we saw the hand of God moving. It is more than ten years later and the church today is one of the fastest growing churches in our community, making a visible impact on the people's lives it serves. To my family I would say, like Joseph, if you did not leave we would not have been where we are. All things worked out for our good.

It is amazing to look back over this period and feel a great sense of gratitude. While going through all of this the feeling of betrayal, rejection and disappointment was just overwhelming. I have grown a lot, we have grown a lot and it is clear to me that these defining moments were crucial to shaping us and they prepared us to get to the Other Side.

Don't be surprised that God is the main orchestrator of most of our detours.

> Then it came to pass, when Pharaoh had let the people go, that God did not lead them by way of the land of the Philistines, although that was near; for God said, "Lest perhaps people change their minds when they see war, and return to Egypt. "**So God led the people around by way** of the wilderness of the Red Sea. And the children of Israel went up in orderly ranks out of the land of Egypt - Exodus 13: 17-18 (NKJV)

With the Israelites leaving Egypt for the promise land, a ten day journey took them forty years. What is interesting about this fact is that God was the main orchestrator of this detour. God was convinced that the Israelites would not make it to the Promised Land taking the shorter route. **There was just too much of Egypt in them to fully comprehend and embrace the Promised Land**. Any major event could make them want to return to what they were used to: Egypt, their place of safety. Egypt, their place of slavery, bondage, and limitation.

When God orchestrates a detour, He has you in mind. Character building and mindset change are in preparation for what God has in store for you. However, I also believe that God did not intend for a ten day journey to take the Israelites forty years. **Their own disobedience and stubbornness made them go around in circles quite a few times.** They themselves were instrumental in creating their own detours, resulting in some of them not even making it to the Promised Land.

Life events outside of your control like the death of a loved one, unfaithfulness of a partner, a failed marriage, a troubled child, an unexpected illness, retrenchment or a failed business, just to mention a few, will in most cases create a detour in your life.

> *To everything thing there is a season, and a time to every purpose under the heaven: A time to be born, and a time to die, a time to plant, and a time to pluck up that which is planted; A time to kill, and a time to heal; a time to break down, and a time to build up. - Ecclesiastes 3:1-3 (KJV)*

When something or someone dies in your life, something new will be born. When something breaks down in your life, it provides the opportunity for something new to be built up. Detours are sometimes God's way of getting us built up and ready for our Other Side. If we do not open ourselves up to learn and grow from our detours, we

GETTING TO THE OTHER SIDE

are destined to repeat them. When you cannot find the purpose in something then "abuse" will be experienced, but when you seek the purpose in something, "use" will be experienced. **We will all need to get to a place where we find the "use" and the "why" for our God given detours.**

Not so long ago I was being groomed to take over the human Resources director role in one of the major companies in South Africa. This grooming process was daunting and intense, one that I subscribed to and sacrificed for. My journey to the Other Side was clearly worked out for me and I was really excited about it. When the opportunity arrived, I came in second with someone from the outside beating me to the post. It was gut wrenching to say the least. What a major reroute! What a major detour! I then decided to leave the corporate world to regroup. The detour became a journey of healing and growth. The time that I spent with my family restored long outstanding issues and allowed us to plan for the next chapter of our lives. The time I spent in ministry allowed the church to hear my heart and it started to grow exponentially. The book that you are reading is part of the fruit of the detour. Thank goodness for the detour, thank goodness for the job disappointment. It contributed to me being where I am today.

God given detours are sometimes good indicators of season changes that are about to take place in your life. Do not despise the detours, but also don't let a good crisis go to waste!

> *But Samuel replied, "What is more pleasing to the LORD: your burnt offerings and sacrifices or your obedience to his voice? Listen! Obedience is better than sacrifice, and submission is better than offering the fat of rams. - 1 Samuel 15:22 (NLT)*

We can make many sacrifices on our way to the Other Side, but what will guarantee us getting there will be our obedience. Disobedience will be the main cause of unnecessary detours that delay your journey. Pride and ego will make you make the same mistakes others have made before you, and will make you go around in circles until you learn some lessons that will set you up for promotion. God requires submission because He knows what He is doing. You also need to submit to people who have gone before you and are already successful in what you are trying to achieve.

We can conclude that detours will be part of your journey to the Other Side. God purposed **detours will shape your character, build your capacity, bring you to a place of humility, renew your mind around certain things, challenge your well worked out plans, deepen your relationship with Him**, and make you more dependent on following His guidance.

Self-inflicted detours will bring you to a **place of frustration and anger. You will start blaming** everyone and everything else around you for where you find yourself today. Submission and obedience will be required to get you back on track.

My brethren, count it all joy when you fall into various trials, knowing that the testing of your faith produces patience. But let patience have its perfect work, that you may be perfect and complete lacking nothing. - James1:2-4 (NKJV)

Happiness is based on experiencing certain happenings while joy is derived from knowing the reason behind the happenings. As you journey to the Other Side, you are guaranteed to fall into some stuff that is not of your own making. The testing of your faith during this time will produce something that you need so that you can complete your journey to the Other Side. Keep the faith and hold on to your joyful demeanor, things will work out for your good.

"GETTING YOU TO THE OTHER SIDE"
GROWTH PLAN
Detour Mastery

LET'S PRAY

Dear heavenly Father I thank You for all the detours in my life. Looking back, I can now see the work that You needed to do in me. This has allowed me to become who I needed to be. Forgive me for all the self-inflicted detours due to my own pride and disobedience. I submit myself to Your will and your ways. In Jesus Name I pray Amen.

Let's get practical:

1. Look back over your life and identify life changing moments that you have experienced as detours. What can you learn from them?
2. How has this helped you to be who you are and where you are today?
3. How will this shape your views around the importance of detours?
4. Can you identify any self-made detours that resulted from your own disobedience?
5. Are you ready to take ownership, repent, and move on?

Let's get an energy boost to help us navigate through our detours

Therefore, since we are surrounded by such a great cloud of witnesses, let us throw off everything that hinders and the sin that so easily entangles. And let us run with perseverance the race marked out for us, fixing our eyes on Jesus, the pioneer and the perfecter of faith. For the joy set before him he endured the cross, scorning its shame, and sat down at the right hand of the throne of God. - Hebrews 12:1-2 (NIV)

But they that wait upon the Lord shall renew their strength; they shall mount up with wings as eagles; they shall run, and not be weary; and they shall walk, and not faint. - Isaiah 40:31 (NKJV)

Trust in the Lord with all your heart and lean not on your own understanding; in all your ways submit to him, and he will make your paths straight. - Proverbs 3:5-6(NIV)

LET'S PRAY

Dear heavenly Father, I say thank You for all the God ordained detours in my life. It is all working out for my good. I will still get to my Other Side. In Jesus Name. Amen

Chapter 8

OVERCOMING THE IMPOSSIBLE

FACING YOUR GIANTS

And David spoke to the men who stood by him, saying, "What shall be done to the man who kills this Philistine and taketh away the reproach from Israel? For who is this uncircumcised Philistine, that he should defy the armies of the living God?' - 1 Samuel 17:26 (KJV)

OVERCOMING THE IMPOSSIBLE

There will come a time that you will discover that the "place" or the destination called the Other Side is so **much bigger than** who **you** are and what you can accomplish by and through your own endeavors. This will become evident when you are faced with giants that will require you to **punch** way **above your weight class**. Sometimes these giants require you to go through them and not just around them. It will require an encounter that you will have to win so that you receive a reward. This prize should **propel you** to your final destination.

Sometimes a real **fight** will be required **to get** you to the **Other Side,** but it is important to fight the fights that you can win, or the ones that you are set up to win. The story of David and Goliath is such a remarkable account of courage and conviction to overcome the odds. David's peers and close relatives did not consider him a giant slayer. This might be true for you when others look at you. People may have already written you off, but just like David, when you know what is at stake you are willing to dig deep, and face the odds, you can start the negotiations for your reward.

Not every fight should be your fight, not every burden is yours to bear. **Choose your fights** wisely. The giant slaying fights will become the most important fights that you will encounter on your way to the

Other Side. Every time you are **feeling small** in the midst of what you are about to face, you are confronted with a **possible giant**. This becomes even more evident when people around you make you feel small based on the criteria that they themselves cannot live up to. When they see the giant that you are facing, knowing that they will not be able to face it themselves, they talk you down hoping that you will shy away and stand defeated. Their biggest fear is not that you will fail or stand defeated, but that you will slay your giant, leaving them with no excuses to do the same.

You can learn a lot from David about when and how to fight so that you can win.

> *Your servant has killed both the lion and the bear; this uncircumcised Philistine will be like one of them, because he has defied the armies of the living God - 1 Samuel 17:36 (NIV)*

David grew up a shepherd boy looking after his father's sheep. A shepherd boy earmarked to become king. It was a farfetched story if there was ever one. What you and I should realize is that everything that we have gone through has been setup to prepare us to slay our giants.

The rural or public school education that David received looking after his father's sheep had prepared him for such a time as this. Goliath received private schooling in the affairs of military warfare and was rated top of his class. **Fighting with the bears and lions prepared David for his Goliath. Don't underestimate what you have been through and where you come from and the informal education that you received in your walk with the Lord.** You can tap into your experiences, victories and personal convictions. The courage to take on the impossible comes from a deep place, a place where you can shout out to everyone around you: "this is me". I know who I am, and I know what I am capable of. This level of confidence comes from a place of personal experience, and education that has evolved into life wisdom where you just know.

So it is time to get ready for the fight. What can we learn from David? *Now the Israelites had been saying, "Do you see how this man keeps coming out? He comes out to defy Israel. The king will give great wealth to the man who kills him. He will also give him his daughter in marriage and will exempt his family from paying taxes. David asked the men standing near him, "What will be done for the man who kills this Philistine and removes this disgrace from Israel? - 1 Samuel 17:25-26 (NIV)*

Firstly, we can learn from David that you should **only go into battle when you are clear about the spoils.** Fighting where there is no reward does not make sense. The battle should also advance your cause to the Other Side. By taking down Goliath, David was assured of proximity to the throne, if this was not so this would be a waste of his time. There will be many obstacles on your way to the Other Side. While this will be so, choose your Goliaths wisely. Stay true to what is important to you, to what you are called to do, fulfilling the requirements as you go along.

I went to university during the Apartheid years in South Africa when we still had a quota system in place, restricting the number of students of color. I remember that on the day of registration, I indicated to my brother who accompanied me, that the university was not for me and we should turn around and go home. I am glad that we stayed and faced the giant of discrimination and segregation. In most classes I attended, we were the minority by far and were made to feel that we did not belong. The education I received changed my life. My way of thinking opened up with so many new avenues to explore. I failed a few subjects in my first and second year, changed a few subjects along the way, but I was still able to finish my first degree in three years. This laid the platform that took me to the highest level in my corporate career and enabled me to scoop an award for the best in my field, nationally.

GETTING TO THE OTHER SIDE

Giants do have an ability to create false evidence; they appear to be real with the main aim of instilling fear that immobilizes you. These giants want you to run for the hills, lash out at yourself or innocent bystanders. However, behind your fear your giant sometimes sits your biggest reward that will accelerate your journey to the Other Side. Fear disappears when you confront it.

Then Saul dressed David in his own tunic. He put a coat of armor on him and a bronze helmet on his head. David fastened on his sword over the tunic and tried walking around, because he was not used to them. "I cannot go in these," he said to Saul, "because I am not used to them." So he took them off. Then he took his staff in his hand, chose five smooth stones from the stream, put them in the pouch of his shepherd's bag and, with his sling in his hand, approached the Philistine - 1 Samuel 17:38-40 (NIV)

When you are ready to face your giants, you will be confronted with the realities of self-imposed limiting beliefs placed there by you or other people. While in most cases the counsel of others is well intended, in some cases what worked for others might not work for you. Stick to what has worked for you in the past. Stick to the life lessons and experience that you have built up. Play to your strengths and play to your advantage. Based on this scripture, there are a few things that we can learn from David and apply when we are facing our giants:

1. Don't fight like your giant. Like for like combat with your giant will guarantee your defeat. Most of our giants are giants in the way that they fight. If you fight in a different way that you are good at, they become small.
2. Your giants biggest strength can be their biggest weakness. David experienced the fact that military armor restricts fast and agile movement. This was true for him and so it will be true for the giant. This allowed David to choose his battle strategy. A sniper cannot miss if the target is slow and stationary. Most of your

giants will not be able to handle your agility. Focus on the "what" and the "why", and be open to the "how". Constantly adjust your "how" until you hit the mark.

Now Eliab his older brother heard when he spoke to the men; and Eliab's anger was aroused against David, and he said, "Why did you come down here? And with whom have you left those few sheep in the wilderness? I know your pride and the insolence of your heart, for you have come down to see the battle." And David said, "What have I done now? Is there not a cause?" - 1 Samuel 17: 28-29 (KJV)

When you make your intentions known - that you are ready to slay your giant, don't be surprised when people very close to you will start to question your intentions. People's accusations and suspicions will be on the rise to try to sway you from facing your giants. Just like David, you are going to have to show resolve and stick to the convictions of your heart. Your biggest challenge is going to be not to pay back anger for anger, but rather to live with the disappointment of others in love and understanding.

So David prevailed over the Philistine with a sling and a stone, and struck the Philistine and killed him. But there was no sword in the hand of David. Therefore, David ran and stood over the Philistine, took his sword and drew it out of its sheath and killed him, and cut of his head with it. And when the Philistines saw their champion was dead, they fled. - 1 Samuel 17:50-51 (NKJV)

Every giant comes with a lot of side noise. When you kill your giant, the noise will also disappear. Be careful not to fight the noise, but rather put your effort and focus on fighting the giant. Always have your mind on the bigger prize, because sometimes we will win the battle, but lose the war.

Just like David, the ultimate goal is to cut the head of the giant. To cut off the mentality of the things facing us is to retract the spoken words that were destined to scare and restrict us.

I can remember a time during my corporate career when I faced the daunting prospect of proposing a culture change program to the Group Executive Team of one of the largest banks. We were convinced that the organization needed a change to respond to the digital transformation happening in the industry. However, the Executive Team was not all on the same page, since the bank was performing very well. "Why fix things when they ain't broken?" For this reason, the proposal we presented received a lot of opposition. I convinced the CEO to give me the opportunity to work with the top 500 executives of the bank to build the case, which he did. Just like David, my name was on the line and I had a lot to lose. However, I knew I was doing the right thing. To cut a long story short, the program that we came up with changed the bank and its response to the digital transformation opportunities. Today this bank is leading on this front relative to its peers. We won the second best team award for the work we did and I was nominated for the CEO Award that year. This silenced my critics and allowed me freedom and support to continue to do some more amazing work.

Punching above your weight class will become a constant requirement as you journey to the Other Side. In some strange way, wherever you may find yourself in life, whatever has happened before has prepared you for what you are facing. Your past is definitely not a representation of your future, but it is definitely your training ground for your future.

One of the modern day giant slayers of our time is the great boxer Manny Pacquiao. Here is his story as related by Wikipedia:

Manny Pacquiao is the only eight-division world champion in the history of boxing, and has won twelve major world titles. He was the first boxer to win the lineal championship in five different weight classes, the first boxer to win major world titles in four of the eight "glamour divisions": flyweight, featherweight, lightweight, and welterweight, and is the only boxer to hold world championships across four decades (1990s, 2000s, 2010s, and 2020s).

As of 2015, Pacquiao's fights had generated $1.2 billion in revenue from his 25 pay-per-view bouts. According to *Forbes*, he was the second highest paid athlete in the world in 2015.

In July 2019, Pacquiao became the oldest welterweight world champion in history at the age of 40, and the first boxer in history to become a recognized four-time welterweight champion after defeating Keith Thurman to win the WBA (Super) welterweight title.

Pacquiao has held the WBA (Super) welterweight title since July 2019. As of August 2020, he is ranked as the world's seventh best active boxer, pound-for-pound, by BoxRec, ninth by Boxing Writers Association of America and tenth by The Ring, ESPN and the Transnational Boxing Rankings Board (TBRB). He is also ranked as the world's second best active welterweight by the TBRB and ESPN, and third by The Ring and BoxRec.

Pacquiao was born and raised in Kibawe, Bukidnon, Philippines. He is the son of Rosalio Pacquiao and Dionisia Dapidran-Pacquiao. His parents separated when he was in sixth grade, after his father had an affair. He is the fourth of six siblings, one of whom, Alberto "Bobby" Pacquiao, is also a politician and former professional boxer.

Pacquiao completed his elementary education at Saavedra Saway Elementary School in General Santos City, but dropped out of high school due to extreme poverty. At the age of 12, Pacquiao was introduced to boxing by his maternal uncle Sardo Mejia. According to his autobiography, Pacquiao said watching Mike Tyson's defeat to James "Buster" Douglas in 1990 with his Uncle Sardo is an experience that, "changed my life forever." His early interest in combat sports was also inspired by martial-artist Bruce Lee and the boxer Muhammad Ali.

GETTING TO THE OTHER SIDE

In 1990, Mejia began training his nephew in a makeshift home gym. After 6 months of training, Pacquiao began boxing in a park in General Santos eventually traveling to other cities to fight higher-ranked opponents. By age 15, he was considered the best junior boxer in the southern Philippines. At the age of 15, he moved to Manila. In January 1995, at the age of 16, he made his professional boxing debut as a junior flyweight.

In February 2007, Pacquiao took and passed a high school equivalency exam, and was awarded with a high school diploma by the Department of Education.

Pacquiao married Jinkee Jamora on May 10, 1999. Together, they have five children, Emmanuel Jr. (Jimuel), Michael Stephen, Mary Divine Grace (Princess), Queen Elizabeth (Queenie) and Israel. His son, Jimuel, is an amateur boxer.His daughter, Queenie, was born in the United States. He resides in his hometown of General Santos City, South Cotabato, Philippines. However, as a congressman of the lone district of Sarangani, he is officially residing in Kiamba, Sarangani, the hometown of his wife.

On December 11, 2019, Pacquiao graduated from University of Makati with a bachelor's degree in political science, majoring in local government administration through the Expanded Tertiary Education Equivalency and Accreditation Program (ETEEAP) of the Philippine Councilors League-Legislative Academy (PCCLA) which allows qualified Filipinos to complete a collegiate-level education via informal education system.

Raised in the Catholic faith, Pacquiao is currently a practicing Evangelical Protestant. Pacquiao said he once had a dream where he saw a pair of angels and heard the voice of God—this dream convinced him to become a devout believer.

OVERCOMING THE IMPOSSIBLE

The modern day life-story of Manny Pacquiao typifies the story of David and Goliath. There are so many similarities. It is time for you to take up your rightful place and position yourself to take down your own giants. Punching above your weight brings with it rewards, privilege, and favor.

What will this fight require from you?

I have fought the good fight, I have finished the race, I have kept the faith. Now there is in store for me the crown of righteousness, which the Lord the righteous Judge, will award to me on that day- not only to me, but also to all who have longed for his appearing. - 2 Timothy 4:7-8 (NIV)

One thing for sure is that **it will be a faith fight**. Tapping into your inner substance and evidence of your experiences as you journey with God will become invaluable to you. Your confidence will come from a deep, assuring, daunting but satisfying place. Having the confidence to see your other side before you get there and making the necessary adjustments in preparation for it, in the here and now is something special to behold. Crazy, but special.

Therefore, I do not run like someone running aimlessly; I do not fight like a boxer beating the air. - 1 Corinthians 9:26 (NIV)

The fight will be a focused fight. Be intentional not to be distracted from what is most important for you to overcome on your way to the other side. Have a clear goal, a clear outcome, or objective. Reserve your energy and resources for the big moments.

The weapons we fight with are not the weapons of the world. On the contrary, they have divine power to demolish strongholds. We demolish arguments and every pretension that sets itself up against the knowledge of God, and we take captive every thought to make it obedient to Christ - 2 Corinthians 10:5 (NIV)

The fight will be a mental one. The battlefield of the mind will become real as your face off against your giants. Your previous programming and experiences will come back to haunt you and you will need to be renewed for you to look at your giants differently. Arguments will be put forward as to why you cannot succeed, why you cannot move forward and your identity in Christ will be the only thing that will keep you sane in the midst of fierce opposition. It will be the right time to dispel the lies spoken over your life and for you to express the truth about who you have become.

For our fight is not against flesh and blood, but against principalities, against powers, against the rules of the darkness of this world, and against spiritual forces of evil in the heavenly places.
- Ephesians 6:12 (MEV)

The fight will be an unseen fight between good and evil. Be of good cheer. Good will always overcome evil, light will always drive out darkness, and love will always overcome fear. Choose to live on the right and bright side of life and you will end up on the winning side more often than you think. Start your unseen fight on your knees as you pray for things and people around you. Don't fight people, but fight what they represent.

"Don't be afraid, "the prophet answered, "Those who are with us are more than those who are with them." And Elisha prayed, "Open his eyes, LORD, so that he may see. "Then the LORD opened the servant's eyes, and he looked and saw the hills full of horses and chariots of fire all around Elisha. - 2 Kings 6:17 (NIV)

The fight will be supported by heaven. We need to be reminded often that we are not alone and that they that are with us are more than them that are against us. We often underestimate that we are fighting God's battles here on earth and every time we commit ourselves to make the world a better place, we team up with heavenly support. Sometimes as servants, we need a prophet to speak healing and hope into our lives as we face our giants, and sometimes we just need to open our eyes and see the invisible hand of God that brought us thus far.

Facing your giants on the way to the Other Side will feel like a title fight. There will be a lot at stake, prepare well, and fight to win.

"GETTING YOU TO THE OTHER SIDE"
GROWTH PLAN
Overcoming The Impossible

Let's get practical:

3. Look back over your life and identify the things that stand in your way for you to get to the Other Side. Based on what you have learned in this chapter, have you changed your mind about your giants? Please explain?
4. How will you go about taking on your giant?
5. What are the rewards for slaying your giant?
6. What will happen if you don't slay your giant?

Let us take in some giant slaying vitamins

So do not fear, for I am with you; do not be dismayed, for I am your God. I will straighten you and help you; I will uphold you with my righteous right hand - Isaiah 41:10

GETTING TO THE OTHER SIDE

Be strong and of good courage, do not fear nor be afraid of them, for the Lord your God, He is the One who goes with you. He will not leave you nor forsake you. - Deuteronomy 31:6

For God has not given us a spirit of fear and timidity, but of power, love, and self-discipline. - 2 Timothy 1:7

David also said to Solomon his son, "Be strong and courageous, and do the work. Do not be afraid or discouraged, for the Lord God, my God is with you. He will not fail you or forsake you until all the work for the service of the temple of the Lord is finished - 1 Chronicles 28:20

LET'S PRAY

Dear heavenly Father I thank You for all the preparation that I have been through so that I can face my giants. I do know that these fights are necessary to take me to my next dimension with you. Going through my giants accelerates my journey to the Other Side, and consolidates who I have become in You. In Jesus Name I pray Amen.

Chapter 9

GROW AS YOU GO

PERSONAL GROWTH WILL BE YOUR PORTION

*And Jesus grew in wisdom and stature, and
in favor with God and man -
Luke 2:52 (NIV)*

GROW AS YOU GO

The way you **measure success** as you journey to the Other Side will play a critical role in you making it there or not. If you are going to measure success purely on the achievements of material things, you are going to be disappointed. The person **who you will be becoming**, and how you relate to others, will be more important than the results you achieve in your life.

The **development of Jesus's character** played such an important role in him finishing his assignment on the cross. He developed wisdom and stature along the way that prepared him for his Other Side. Based on his **character development**, he **received the support** from heaven and from people around him. The one thing that people **cannot take away** from you is **your personal growth**, and the more capacity you acquire, the more things you will need in your life will be added to you. **True wealth sits within your capacity to be and to do.**

The greatest joy on your journey to the Other Side will be who you are becoming. Be prepared that the person who started this journey will not be the same person on the Other Side.

The parable of the talents is a great example of the important role that personal development will play in your life.

> *To one he gave five bags of gold, to another two bags, and to another one bag, **each according to his ability**. Then he went on his journey. The man who received five bags of gold went at once and put his money to work, and gained five bags more. The man who received five bags of gold brought the other five. "Master, he said, you entrusted me with five bags of gold. See I gained five more." His master replied, **"Well done, good and faithful servant.** You have been faithful with a few things; I will put you in charge over many things. Come and share you master's happiness!" - Matthew 25:21 (NIV)*

Entrustment of things is **correlated** to your **personal growth** and development. Being put in charge of things will depend on your capacity to grow and take care of it. Living your life to its fullest potential will create the capacity to bring about a hundred percent return with the promise of being entrusted with more. It is interesting to note that being **entrusted** to your **fullest potential** God sees as **being faithful with the little**. Even more so, **God** is **moved** when you are **faithful at the beginning,** when things are still small. When the production is minimal, when the business idea is at its inception phase, when you are just getting over some stuff, when it is at the beginning of a relationship, when you need to make sacrifices to learn or venture into something new, and when you need to hone in your craft or talent in front of small crowds. Faithfulness with the little will always bring you to a place of plenty. **When you are faithful with the little, you open yourself up to grow your capacity to attract the bounteous.**

This passage also reminds us that God is more concerned about our **character development**, "good and faithful" that receives a "well done" from Him, as this will lay the **foundation for achieving future success.**

Being put in charge and becoming a shareholder of what will unfold in the future will bring you to a place where you will experience frequent happiness.

So the question that you should sit with is: **How do I develop my character and my abilities?** How do I develop the distinctive mental and moral qualities that I would need to carry me to the Other Side? How do I continue to grow in how I relate and what I am able to do?

Like anything else, where there is no purpose neglect and abuse will take place. There must be a purpose behind your character development, a greater cause that you stand for or represent, something or someone that you are **standing in service of**. Who you are **becoming will always be more important** than what you are achieving.

God has a **vested interest** in your **personal development**. He is aware that your personal growth is an important part in your obtaining the inheritance that He has in store for you. With this in mind, He has committed Himself to be an active contributor and participant in your development. However, you are going to have to do your part and God will do his.

> *But you will **receive power** when the Holy Spirit comes on you; and **you will be** my witnesses in Jerusalem, and in all Judea and Samaria, and to the ends of the earth." - Acts 1:8 NIV)*

God's **greatest contribution** is to **empower you** to do the assignment that He has placed over your life. He has not called you to the Other Side without giving you the tools to do so. Empowerment to do is very close to God's heart. A big part of your **development** will be your willingness to **receive from God His empowerment** for you to be and to do.

The Oxford Dictionary defines empowerment as "**authority** or **power given** to someone **to do something**; the **process of becoming** stronger and more **confident**, especially in controlling one's life and **claiming one's rights.**"

There are certain things that you will have to develop along the way, **a process of becoming**, and there are certain things that you **just have to receive**. It is amazing to see how a traffic officer can stop a big truck or direct traffic by using hand signals. The uniform and badge gives officers certain powers and authority to do what they do. This is true for the traffic officer as it is true for you. You get authority from who you are in Christ and power from the person of the Holy Spirit. Both privileges can be accessed by faith, not something you can work for, but something that you need to open up your heart to and receive.

Authority has a lot to do with your **identity**. When you know who you are, you will become more comfortable to do what you need to do. It is quite sad to see that most of us are on this rat race of believing that what we do and what we achieve will make us who we are. You have to shift from "what you do makes you who you are" to "who you are makes you do what you do."

> *Before I formed you in the womb, I knew you (and approved of you as My chosen instrument). And before you were born I consecrated you (to Myself as My own); I have appointed you as a prophet to the nations." - Jeremiah 1:5 (Amplified)*

Your approval, acceptance, and significance over your life sit with the **One who Created** you. He sorted that out even before you made your entrance here on earth. You being here has just put flesh to a planned destiny that God has over your life. The content and context that you are born into makes unique ingredients for you to speak from an authentic voice that is deeply connected to your spiritual convictions. **It is interesting to see how we have allowed our life experiences to erode our approval, acceptance, and our**

significance. The biggest pain we will experience in our lifetime will be the dissonance we experience when we live a life outside what we are designed to be. While SIN (**S**omeone **I** am **N**ot) has become the main culprit to create dissonance, Christ came so that we can find our pre-created self in Him.

*There are **different kinds** of **gifts**, but the **same Spirit** distributes them. There are different kinds of **service**, but the **same Lord**. There are different kinds of **working**, but it all of them and in everyone it is the **same God** at work. Now to each one the **manifestation** of the Spirit is given for the **common good.** - 1 Corinthians 12:4-7 (NIV)*

God has made sure to bless you with a supernatural endowment that will enable you to **serve,** to **work**, and to **manifest** things in your lifetime for the **common good** of men. Your giftedness will be a sign that you have been given a special assignment that has been mandated and enabled by God Himself. You are born with an assignment. People have created that our life journey is about figuring out our assignments. This prevents and delays the work that we need to do here on earth.

*Now when the men of the Sanhedrin (Jewish High Court) **saw** the **confidence** and the **boldness** Peter and John, grasped **the facts** that they were **uneducated and untrained** (ordinary) men, they were astounded, and began to **recognize** that they **had been with Jesus**. - Acts 4:13*

When it comes to your **development,** it is all about having the **confidence** and the **boldness to be** who you are and do what you are supposed to do. What happens when someone has been with Jesus is amazing, even the uneducated and untrained men are able to demonstrate abilities that they have not been schooled for. This **supernatural endowment** creates a stir that directs people back to Him who has given you this ability. So, it is important to recognise that God has given you supernatural abilities that come with your assignment here on earth. However, that is half of the endowment;

the **other half** will come from you **developing yourself** in areas that you will require to fulfill and complete your journey to the Other Side.

*Saul replied, "You are not able to go out against this **Philistine** and fight for him; you are only a young man, and he has been a **warrior from his youth**." However, **David** said to Saul, "Your servant has been keeping his father's sheep. When a lion or a bear came and carried off a sheep from the flock, I went after it, struck, and killed it. Your servant has **killed both the lion and the bear**; this uncircumcised Philistine will be one of them, because he had defied the armies of the living God. - 1 Samuel 17:34-36(NIV)*

The story of David and Goliath reminds us of the **importance of informal education.** Saul reminded David that Goliath went through formal military training from a young age and for that reason David would stand no chance against him. David was quick to pull on his credentials of the informal "lion and bear" training he went through while looking after his father's sheep. It is important to look back over your life and see what your life experiences have taught you and how this has prepared you for such a time as this. This is true for both your personal, professional, and spiritual life.

*The things (the doctrine, the precepts, the admonitions, the **sum of my ministry**) which you have **heard me teach** in the presence of many witnesses, **entrust** (as a treasure) to **reliable** and **faithful** men who will also be **capable** and **qualified** to **teach others**. - 2 Timothy 2:2 (Amplified)*

God's entrustment over your life **will depend** on your **character development** rooted in your reliability, your faithfulness, and your capability development confirmed through **qualifications or public endorsement**. What holds this together will be **your teachability** or learning agility as some may call it; your ability to take instruction and feedback from others and to avail yourself to teach and mentor others. As you journey to the Other Side; you have to **see yourself**

as a brand. A personal brand that will attract entrustment for what is needed to get you to the Other Side. How reliable are you? How faithful are you to what is important to you? Are you open to learn from others and to share what you already know?

Let us dig a little deeper into our understanding of our abilities as we journey to the other side.

Ability is a possession of the **means** or **skill** to do something, **talent** or **proficiency** in a particular area. (Oxford online dictionary)

Wherever you are going, you will need to have the means to get there, or at least be able to attract the means to get there. You will need to **embrace** and work with the **gifts and talents** that God has blessed you with, **develop** the necessary **skills** through formal or informal learning experiences, and **focus** on a particular area that you can **become really good at;** in other words highly proficient.

A man's gift makes room for him, And brings him before great men,
- Proverbs 18:16 (NKJV)

What you bring to the table will **open doors** for you. Who you bring will relate to your character, how you bring it will relate to your ability, and what you bring will relate to your capability. What you bring to your personal, professional or spiritual life will open the necessary opportunities, **who you bring ,and how you bring** it will determine **how long you will stay** to benefit from these opportunities.

Again, it is important to reiterate that you should use your personal development as the ultimate measure of your success. Whoever and whatever you become will attract what you need for your journey to the Other Side.

This reminds me of a time when I was in my late twenties. I decided to leave my corporate job to start my own business in the people development space. This allowed me to venture into areas that I always wanted to, working with clients from various sectors. The exposure was great and I learned a lot about being an entrepreneur, customer service, consulting, and product development, just to mention a few. After being in business for three years, the business went through a bad patch and we lost everything. Regret crept in and I started to ask myself if I had made the right call to leave my corporate career. When I looked at my peers that I left behind most of them had become even more successful and that made matters worse.

In a strange turn of events, the same organisation approached me to apply for a vacancy that they had. They were so impressed by the experience I gained working for various sectors that they offered me a very senior position equivalent or even higher than those held by my previous peers. The salary package that came with it allowed me to sort out our debt over a very short time. This opportunity enabled me to become a multimillionaire before I turned forty.

So we have spoken about your character, your gifts, your talents and the skills required to get you to the Other Side, but what about your personality?

What are the **combinations** of **characteristics** or qualities that form your **distinctive character**? These traits are normally formed during the first seven years of your life, and will bring character to the instrument that God will use. God is not in the business of changing your character, but using it. **He is** however **keen** to change and **supplement** the **essence** of your character.

> *Meanwhile, Saul was still breathing out murderous threats against the Lord's disciples. He went to the high priest and asked him for letters to the synagogues in Damascus so that if he found any there who belonged to the Way, whether men or women, he might take then as prisoners to Jerusalem. - Act 9:1-2(NIV)*

GROW AS YOU GO

But the Lord said to Ananias, "Go! This man is my chosen instrument to proclaim my name to the Gentiles and their kings and to the people of Israel. - Act 9:15(NIV)

Saul who later became Paul had a driver, driver personality. He was task driven and an overachiever of note to get things done, which he believed in, and was assigned to. God wanted to use the same personality that was destroying the Church to promote it. This was true for Paul as it is for you. God wants to use your personality.

Our personalities are formed primarily during the first seven years of our lives and shape the wiring that will take place over the rest of our lives. God is aware of your personality and has no need to change it. Every personality type sits with positives and negatives, and the negatives make us question the usefulness of our personalities to get us to the Other Side.

But the fruit of the Spirit is love, joy, peace, forbearance, kindness, goodness, faithfulness, gentleness and self-control. Against such things, there is no law. - Galatians 5:22-23

God has made provision to **compensate** and **complement** for our **personality deficiencies**. When we stay close to Him and allow the Holy Spirit to work in us we will produce fruits that will complement, compensate, and sometimes supersede our personality type to bring about the required change that will get us to the Other Side.

"GETTING YOU TO THE OTHER SIDE"
GROWTH PLAN
Grow As You Go Mastery

LET'S PRAY

Dear Heavenly Father I thank you for all the gifts and talents that you have blessed me with. I am grateful for all the formal and informal opportunities that you have given me to acquire skills that will benefit me and others along the way. Thank you for the people that shaped my early life and helped me to form my personality. I am grateful for the Holy Spirit that is producing fruits that help me to exhibit myself in a way that I can be a blessing to others. In Jesus Name I pray Amen.

Let's get practical:

1. As you look over your life, what gifts and talents are you blessed with?
2. What skills have you acquired that you are quite proud of?
3. What will you have to get better at, if you are going to get to the Other Side?
4. What exposure and experience do you need to develop these abilities?
5. Who are the people that you can learn from?
6. What formal education or training will be useful to develop these abilities?

7. Let us take in some personal development nuggets:

Making the most of every opportunity, because the days are evil. - Ephesians 5:16

Being confident of this, that he who had began a good work in you will carry it on to completion until the day of Christ Jesus. - Philippians 1:6

So then, just as you received Christ Jesus as Lord, continue to live your lives in him, rooted and built up in him, strengthened in faith as you were taught, and overflowing with thankfulness. - Colossians 2:6-7

CLOSING PRAYER

Thank you Lord that I will continue to grow as I go. My growth will determine my level of entrustment. I am open to learning from the experiences and opportunities You direct me to. In Jesus name, Amen.

Chapter 10

HELPING OTHERS ALONG THE WAY

BUILDING STRONG RELATIONSHIPS

Jesus called them together and said, "You know that the rulers of the Gentiles lord over them, and their high officials exercise authority over them, Not so with you. Instead, whoever wants to become great among you must be your servant. - Matthew 20:25-26 (NIV)

HELPING OTHERS ALONG THE WAY

Sometimes people mistake getting to the Other Side as something they can achieve by destroying others along the way. They consider it as the easiest route. No emotional attachments, no relationship building, just pure transactional, "let us get the job done". We are living in a time where the mindset that says, "The end justifies the means" is prevalent. However, the scripture reminds us that true greatness is developed when you present yourself in service to others. **Getting to the Other Side will sometimes require you to get things done through others and in most cases through help from others,** so it is important that you genuinely help others along the way. It helps you to develop much needed greatness that will get you to the Other Side.

Great people are service-oriented, great businesses are service-oriented . Above average businesses sit with the added x-factor of extra-ordinary service. You can sit with the same business, sell the same product, but your orientation service that will be your key differentiator.

Why will service orientation make you great? When you take on a service-oriented disposition, you are on the outlook to meet and service the needs of others through the service that you render. Compassion and empathy for others become the key drivers for you to stay relevant, continuously growing in your craft as you journey to the Other Side. It also keeps you humble as you remain open to feedback that makes who you are and what you do better. You will achieve greatness when you make a shift from others servicing you to you getting others to serve a cause or a goal that is far greater than you are. God guaranteed greatness when you stand in service of a great cause, backed up by a Great God. When you get others enrolled into service, you provide them the very same opportunity to find their sweet spot of greatness.

Self-interest will create the need for you to lord over others and to exercise authority over them in pursuit of selfish goals. While this might work for some time, as soon as the cost versus benefit ratio for the people following or supporting you does not make sense, they will leave or at most they will stay and do the bare minimal. **Helping others along the way is not just a good idea; it is a great idea.**

*God blessed them and said to them, "Be **fruitful** and **increase** in number; fill the earth and subdue it. Rule over the fish in the sea and the birds in the sky and over every living creature that moves on the ground" - Genesis 1:28 (NIV)*

*The LORD God said, "It's not good for the **man to be alone**, I will make a **helper suitable** for him" - Genesis 2:18 (NIV)*

You can never reach the places of fruitfulness and increase alone. In most cases you will need the help of suitable others to get you to the Other Side. So, intentionally manage your relationships. Who is in, who is out, whom you should invest in, and who should invest in you, should be top of your mind. The quality of your relationships will make or break you. Being out of balance in your relationship will slow down your progress. If most of the people that you are connected to need your help, and you do not have enough people that can help you along the way, you will soon experience a burnout that will slow down your progress to the Other Side.

HELPING OTHERS ALONG THE WAY

Two are better than one, because they have a good return for their labor, if either of them falls down, one can help the other up. But pity anyone who falls and has no one to help them up. Also if two lie together, they will keep warm. But how can one keep warm alone? Though one may be overpowered, two can defend themselves. A chord of three strands is not quickly broken.
- Ecclesiastes 4:9-12 (NIV)

The above scripture is a great reminder of the benefits of doing things with others. However, it is obvious that it must be with the "right others". Developing strong relationships on your journey to the Other Side will be non-negotiable. Your relationship skills cannot be at the same level at the start of your journey as at the end. If you are going to make it to the Other Side, your quality, and growth in relationships will play a significant role. Helping others and others helping you will be a key hallmark of your journey. **Some people will stay for a season, and some will stay for a lifetime. However, you becoming better at relationships will add more richness, colour, depth, personal growth, progress, and productivity, as you journey to the Other Side.**

When they had done so, they caught such a large number of fish that their nets began to break. So they signaled their partners in the other boat to come and help them, and they came and filled both boats so full that they began to sink. - Luke 5:6-7(NIV)

Being connected to the right people at the right time can be a life-changing moment. Choosing the right partners where mutual exchange of value exists can raise the odds of your success. If you succeed, your partners succeed, and if your partners succeed, you succeed.

Nevertheless, you also need people to stand with you through difficult times. **You need people to see what you see, acknowledge the genuineness of your cause, invest time and resources in you,**

knowing that eventually you will succeed in your endeavours. The same people who were with Peter when he succeeded were the same people who stood by him when he toiled all night and caught nothing. You will need to build genuine partnerships with others if you are going to make it to your Other Side. If you want to go somewhere quickly, go alone, and if you want to go far in life, take others with you.

So how do I become better at building strong and lasting relationships?

> *And the second is like it, Love your neighbor as you love yourself - Matthew 22:39(NIV)*

Many of our relationships with others are a reflection of the love we have for ourselves. Our relationships with things or people are serving us in one way or the other. Our lack of self-love can make us connect to things or people that will feed that void. This will normally usher in a doorway of stagnation or destruction. Where a lack of self-love exists, normally abuse will be present; abuse of substance or abuse in relationships. If you want to be good at relationships, you will have to practice self-love or as some call it "self-care". This does not promote self-centeredness or selfishness, but self-care. You cannot give away what you don't have, and the quality of relationships you have with things and people is a clear reflection of the love you have for yourself. **Being in relationships where you constantly seek and crave the approval of others is a reflection that you lack approval within yourself.**

We however sit with the dilemma that a product or creation cannot bestow approval on itself or oneself. The approval must come from the manufacturer or the creator. God himself can only bestow so authentic self-love upon us. Having an authentic and genuine relationship with your Creator will be the best thing you can do to restore your self-love.

> *__Before I formed you__ in the womb I knew you (and __approved of you__ as My chosen instrument), And before you were born I consecrated you (to Myself as My own); I have appointed you as a prophet to the nations - Jeremiah 1:5 (AMP)*

God gave us our approval before we entered the earth. We are here on an assignment.

Like most things in life if you don't have the "why" for something, misuse or abuse will happen. This is true for most things and relationships. Why do you stand in certain relationships? How does that relate to who you are and who you are becoming? What has been entrusted to you as part of this relationship that you need to fight for to preserve? What are the roles that you have to play in order to preserve this relationship? What day-to-day tasks do you have to commit to, to make a meaningful contribution to this relationship? When do you know it is time to exit this relationship?

> *There is a season (a time appointed) for everything and a time for every delight and event or purpose under heaven*
> *- Ecclesiastes 3:1 (AMP)*

This is true for life as it is true for our relationships.

Once you have made progress on the above, you are encouraged to live by the golden rule of life.

> *So in everything, do to others what you would have them do to you, for this sums up the Law and the Prophets - Matthew 7:12 (NIV)*

Whatever you expect others to do for and to you in relationships, do it first to them. Be the friend, be the husband or wife, be the business partner, be the employee, or employer that you would like to have and you will be surprised by what you will get in return. To build strong and enduring relationships we need to move away from "what are my rights" to "what are my responsibilities to make this relationship work". Once you have done all things to stand in a relationship and you are not getting the necessary return, this will indicate that it is time for you to re-evaluate the thing or person that you are standing in relationship with.

My dear brothers and sisters take note of this: Everyone should be quick to listen, slow to speak and slow to become angry
- James 1:19 (NIV)

Living in understanding with others will require you to raise your level of listening. First seek to understand, before being understood will go a long way in building lasting relationships. We, however, must not confuse understanding with agreement. You need to understand where someone is coming from to be able to respond in a meaningful and constructive way even if you do not agree with their actions or behaviour. Being slow to speak reminds us of the importance of considering our words especially when the moment demands it from us. During crucial moments, reserve your judgment, ask open-ended questions to find out more, and do not take things personally, as this will invite offense into your heart. Once you understand a situation, you can add value to it.

Improve your level of listening, from listening to what you want to hear, to becoming more curious about differences, to listening from a place of empathy. The importance of listening also highlights the importance of feedback that you receive. Listen for what is not being said, listen between the lines, what are people trying to say to you. Take the feedback that will help you to align your behaviour to your intentions, and disregard feedback that attacks your character.

While there are many things to consider in building lasting mutually beneficial relationships, the above will get you a long way. Lastly, we need to be clear on the role that we need to play in the lives of others when it comes to relationships. At the start of this chapter, we were reminded that we needed to **fight against the need to want to control others for our benefit** or to make us look good, but rather to focus on the needs of others and how we can be of service to them.

If there is anyone that you are going to have to control in building lasting relationships, it will be yourself. Self-control is such an essential attribute that you will have to exercise. Reserving your judgement, developing understanding for where others are, so that you will be able to respond to situations and not just react, will ensure that your relationships stay healthy and productive. This will even provide you with the opportunity to speak the truth in love when the situation demands it. The truth will sometimes hurt, but when spoken from a place of love, it will be embraced as part of growing up.

*Whoever has **no rule over his own spirit**, is like a **city broken down**, without walls. - Proverbs 26:28(NKJV)*

*Instead, speaking the **truth in love**, **we will grow** to become in every respect the **mature** body of him who is the head, that is, Christ. - Ephesians 4:15(NIV)*

The above chapter reminds me of my marriage relationship. At the time of writing this book, we are about to celebrate our twentieth year anniversary. Over the twenty years, I have come to realise that there is no such thing as a broken marriage, but just two broken individuals who got married. The prevailing mantra in some marriages is, "In our marriage more me than my wife". The real design of marriage is to create a conducive environment for two individuals to work together to find healing and grow together based on a shared purpose and vision.

I was a very controlling at the start of our marriage due to my own insecurities and lack of self-love. This nearly destroyed what God has put together. Some of what I discussed in this chapter helped me along the way. I am no more the man I used to be and marriage has helped me to become a better version of myself. God-ordained relationships are designed to make you better; however, you need to be willing to part of the growing and maturing process.

"GETTING YOU TO THE OTHER SIDE"
GROWTH PLAN
Building Lasting Relationships

LET'S PRAY

Dear heavenly Father I thank you for all the people that you have placed in my life. This I pray for my personal, professional, and spiritual life. I pray that you will continue to give me wisdom and guidance as to how I should regulate my relationship with things and people for the benefit of the mandate that you have placed over life. Grant me grace to continue to grow in my relationships. In Jesus Name I pray Amen.

Let's get practical:

1. Take a blank piece of paper and make a small circle in the middle of the page with your name in it. Label the page either Personal/Professional/Spiritual.
1. Make and connect circles all around it; illustrate all the relationships that you have in that area of your life as well as its importance by the size of the circle.

2. Put a +/- next to each circle and write down what is working and not working in each of these relationships.
3. Pray over each one of your relationship and write down what you are going to do about it to make it to make it even better.
4. Envision what you want it to look like and why?
5. Go back to the middle of your page and write next to your name what relationships you would need going forward and where you need to walk away from.
6. Do the same for the next area of your life. Remember that you also stand in relationship with things as well as with people.

Let us take in some relationship development nuggets:

Better a patient person than a warrior, one with self-control than one who takes a city - Proverbs 16:32

Do not be misled "Bad company corrupts good character" - 1 Corinthians 15:33 (NIV)

Therefore, encourage one another and build one another up, just as you are doing - 1 Thessalonians 5:11

I therefore, a prisoner for the Lord, urge you to walk in a manner worthy of the calling to which you have been called, with all humility and gentleness, with patience, bearing with one another in love, eager to maintain the unity of the Spirit in the bond of peace - Ephesians 4:1-3

LET'S PRAY

Lord continue to expand my life through my relationships. In Jesus Name. Amen

Chapter 11

TRUST THE MASTER NAVIGATOR

THE ROLE OF THE PERSON OF THE HOLY SPIRIT

But when he, the Spirit of truth comes, He will guide you into all truth. He will not speak on his own; He will speak only what He hears, and will tell you what is yet to come. - John 16:13 (NIV)

TRUST THE MASTER NAVIGATOR

Life always has a way to surprise you. Encountering the supernatural will remind you that **a bigger force is ultimately in charge of your outcome**. Getting to the Other Side will require someone bigger than you to guide you; someone who is aware of what is to come.

When we do talk about supernatural people, we are quickly put off by it due to how it has been portrayed. However, the Bible reminds us that the **Holy Spirit is a Person** who wants to have a personal relationship with us. He will play the role of **revealing the truth** to you and will play the role of **master navigator who brings divine protection.** This assurance over your life gives you a great sense of comfort that what you are to set out to do has heaven's endorsement.

This reminds me of a time when the Holy Spirit woke me up at 2:00am warning me that people were about to break into our house. After wrestling with Him for a few minutes with what I heard, I eventually got up to check the back door of our house that was beneath our bedroom window. While I was looking down there, I did not see anyone. As I continued to investigate, three thugs came around the corner and were shocked to find me waiting for them. I had startled them and they ran off. My life would have been different if they had the opportunity to enter our home.

GETTING TO THE OTHER SIDE

We do have the **privilege to have the Holy Spirit** in our lives to tell us of things to come. To warn us and sometimes even to direct us especially when life does not make sense. We all come to a place in our lives where we have done all that we can do to get us to the Other Side, and sometimes it just feels like it is not enough. When those moments arise, we can either give up or start to **tap into the relationships that we have with the Holy Spirit**. The Holy Spirit will reveal the **truth** in the midst of lies and give you **guidance** when you cannot see the way ahead of you; he **will allow** you to continue to **move forward**.

We were very excited when we got the news that my wife was pregnant with our first child. Half-way through the pregnancy the doctor gave us the bad news that our child was not growing as she should and this would cause complications at birth. As we stepped out of the doctor's office both of us were convicted that things would work out well and we immediately laid hands on our child and prayed for her.

As the pregnancy progressed, it was quite clear that a cesarean birth would be required and that the doctor who treated us needed to be the one to do it. When the time arrived for my wife to go into labour, I rushed her to hospital at 12:00am in the morning. When we entered the hospital premises, armed robbers entered behind us. As I booked my wife into her ward and returned to the administration area to complete the paperwork, the armed robbers confronted me; they were ransacking the hospital. I returned to my wife's side and waited for the doctor to arrive while the hospital was in lockdown.

As the time of delivery drew near the hospital could not get hold of our doctor, and they needed to use the doctor who was on stand-by. He arrived and without any complications, he just delivered the baby through normal birth. Today our baby is seventeen years old, a head girl of a prestigious school in our area, an A student in Maths and Science, a gifted singer and worshiper, passionate about life, and someone destined to make her mark.

Opening yourself up to the **revelation, conviction** and **communication** of the **Holy Spirit** on your way to the Other Side will be one of the most memorable and profound experiences that you will have.

By doing this, you are acknowledging that you don't know everything and that you will need guidance from above.

> *And I will ask the Father, and He will give you another **Helper (Comforter, Advocate, Intercessor, Counselor, Strengthener, Standby**) to be with you forever, the Spirit of Truth, whom the world cannot receive (and take to its heart) because it does not see Him or know him. but you know Him because he (the Holy Spirit) remains with you continually and will be with you. - John 14:6-7 (AMP)*

The **Holy Spirit** is there to **help**, and to be quite honest, we need all the help that we can get. The above passage elaborates the different helping roles that the Holy Spirit will play in our lives: that of a comforter, a counselor, an advocate, and a praying partner. Most of these roles will help us to make better decisions going forward and ensure that we get to the Other Side.

Quite a few years ago, my wife and I were in the market to purchase a day-care centre. We prayed about it and went about to scout for one in various 'businesses for sale' online platforms and magazines. We spotted one that we were interested in and after seeing it, we decided to make an offer. On our way back, we still felt a level of discomfort about our purchase, as it was not exactly what we wanted, but it was the best one we had seen.

Back home while drinking coffee and talking about our purchase, the Holy Spirit prompted me to open a property magazine that was laying on the table. To our surprise, a day-care centre, within walking distance from our home, in pristine condition, and ideally situated was for sale. We immediately contacted the agent, saw the property the same day, made the offer and the rest is history. We were able to cancel the previous purchase by paying a small penalty. Today that school is a thriving business in every sense of the word.

Purchasing the first property would have been a grave mistake that would have cost us a lot of money and caused misery. I am grateful to the Holy Spirit for His guidance.

The Holy Spirit does not only play a role in your life when things turn out well, but **He also helps when you go through your darkest hour. Comfort** does not prevent you from going through pain, but helps you to make sense of your pain. **It cushions you so that you can bear it and make sense of it.**

Not long ago, I lost my Dad to cancer. He was very close to my immediate family and me; we shared very profound moments together, especially in the later part of his life. You see, I was his Pastor, responsible for the well-being of his soul. My father grew up very poor and needed to fend for himself from a very young age. This made him wise in so many aspects of life, but it also came with addictions that tormented him for most of his life. I saw him struggle; searching for answers, trying to overcome his character flaws.

Two years before his passing, he experienced a major breakthrough in his life at a Bible study where for the first time he grasped who he was in Christ. God gave him a new identity and he was willing to receive it. This totally changed my Dad and it was evident for everyone to see. A few months before his passing, he started complaining of severe coughing. My sister-in law took him to the doctor, he was diagnosed with pneumonia, and they treated him accordingly.

When his condition did not improve, I asked him to come and stay with me so that we could keep an eye on him. We spent some quality time together talking about life and he shared with me that he was ready to go home. While this was not what I wanted to hear, the Holy

Spirit confirmed and comforted me in a way that prepared me for the journey ahead.

My father's condition got worse and I rushed him to hospital, where they connected him to oxygen to help with his breathing. After doing extensive tests they discovered he had stage four lung cancer and he did not have long to live.

On receiving the news, my Dad continued to exhibit amazing peace, demonstrating a great sense of humor, sharing his last words of what he expected from his family going forward. During that time, I experienced my Dad as an Angel talking to us. It was not long after that, my Dad said goodbye to us with an amazing smile and contentment on his face. With this sense of comfort, I preached at my father's funeral giving him the send-off sermon that he deserved. After all, I was his pastor.

The grief and the mourning for my Dad did not last very long, but the impact that he made in my life and in my family's life still lingers on. He also made a huge impact in fathering the fatherless in the community where he stayed and within our church where he served. I still hear his name being mentioned in the corridors of our church when we talk about the positive impact an imperfect Dad had on so many lives.

The comfort of the Holy Spirit gives perspective in the most difficult moments in our lives. He helps us to draw strength and wisdom so that we can carry on, on our way to the Other Side.

Don't underestimate the guidance, protection, and comfort the Holy Spirit provides when we need it the most. All the above makes me conclude that God has a planned destiny for our lives and we need the Master Navigator, the Holy Spirit, to get us there.

"GETTING YOU TO THE OTHER SIDE"
GROWTH PLAN
The Role Of The Person Of The Holy Spirit

LET'S PRAY

Dear Heavenly Father I thank you for never leaving me nor forsaking me. I invite and recognize the Person of the Holy Spirit in my life that will guide and protect me on my way to the Other Side. Allow me to hear His voice when I am confronted with things and decisions I don't understand. In Jesus name, I pray Amen.

Let's Get Practical:

But the spiritual man (the spiritually mature Christian) judges all things **(questions, examines and applies what the Holy Spirit reveals)**, *yet is himself judged by no one (the unbeliever cannot judge and understand the believer's spiritual nature) - 1 Corinthians 2:15 (AMP)*

1. Look at areas or situations in your life where you need guidance from God as you are not making much progress?
1. Pray for that situation and open yourself up for the guidance of the Holy Spirit.
2. Search for a few scriptures that speak about your situation. Read them out loud and pray about it.
3. Pose some questions about your situation such as, "Why it is what it is."
4. Ask God to examine your heart and your situation and give you confirmation about the way forward.
5. Put into action what God is speaking to you about as He starts to reveal things to you.

Chapter 12

GET READY FOR THE OTHER SIDE

PLAN FOR YOUR EXPANSION

Now unto Him who is able to do exceedingly abundantly above all that we ask or think, according to the power that works in us
- Ephesians 3:20 (NKJV)

GET READY FOR THE OTHER SIDE

We have made it to the last chapter of this book. What a ride, what a journey to the Other Side. You will soon discover that shifts are starting to take place in your life and that you are not the only one at work. Once you create momentum in pursuit of your God-given purpose, destiny, and design, you leave God with no option but to lend a hand. When He gets involved, He always exceeds our expectations. Things will not always work out the way you would like them to work out, but with God, it always works out better. During the course of this journey you have asked, thought, reflected and did a lot. However, it has dawned on you that certain things are just beyond your human abilities, and some things just happened for you without you lifting a finger.

Becoming and doing more is God's way of preparing you for expansion. God is busy working in you and through you to set you up for His expansion plan. Getting you to the Other Side is (in most cases) not your final destination, but the start of a brand new one. With your renewed competence and confidence gained, you will soon realise that you will be facing new and exciting seasons in your life. Whatever you have been through has in some way prepared you to be who you are, where you are, and for you to do what you do.

GETTING TO THE OTHER SIDE

Coming from a home where my parents were divorced and struggling with the notion of marriage, little did I know that God would use me and my family to stand in ministry to help and restore many marriages and homes today.

Suffering with addiction most of my teen and young adult life, little did I know that this will open a door for me to minister and restore people who are suffering from addictions.

Growing up as a very shy and insecure boy, little did I know that I will help people today to find their unique voice. Once you get to the other side of things, don't be surprised by the new open doors that will await you.

*Therefore see that you **walk carefully** (living with **honor, purpose,** and **courage, shunning** those who tolerate and enable evil), not as the unwise, but as the wise (**sensible, intelligent, discerning people**), **making the very most of your time** (on earth, recognizing and taking advantage of each opportunity and using it with wisdom and diligence), because the days are (filled with) evil*
- Ephesians 5:15-16 (AMP)

It is so important that you keep on walking. While life will require you to take time out to rest, timeout for renewal, timeout for healing and restoration, it is important that you do that with the intention to keep on moving forward. Nothing will keep you moving forward like your purpose in life. Why you are here will be your ultimate driving force that will get you up in the morning even if you do not feel like it, to take on more and to expand, even if it does not make sense.

Shunning things that keep you away from your destiny and keeping your heart clean from unbelief will allow you to remain present every day so that you can make use of every opportunity that lies ahead of you. Living day-by-day, knowing that how well you live today will have a profound impact on your tomorrow will require you to end each day knowing that you have done your best for that day. We are encouraged not to live today with yesterday in mind as this will rob us of today and it will impact our tomorrow.

> *So do not worry about tomorrow, for tomorrow will worry about itself. Each day has enough trouble of its own.*
> *- Matthew 6:34 (AMP)*

Bringing yesterday's or tomorrow's worries into today will rob you of today. Expansion is seeing the opportunities presented to you every day to make a unique contribution that will set you up for tomorrow. A better today will ensure a better tomorrow. So be intentional about your day, as far as you can, every day.

On my 30th birthday, my wife decided to take me out on a very expensive romantic dinner to celebrate. She even bought me a special outfit for the occasion. While we were sitting down, surrounded by a romantic ambiance, I uttered the words looking into my wife's eyes: "What are we going to do tomorrow." That ruined the evening. I have come to realise after twenty years of marriage that being present and making the most of every occasion, helps you to experience expansion in marriage.

> *When he had finished speaking, he said to Simon, "Put out into **deep water**, and let down the nets for a catch," Simon answered, "Master, we've **worked hard** all night and haven't caught anything. But because you say so, I will let down the nets. When they had done so, they **caugh**t such a **large number** of fish that their nets began to break. So they **signaled their partners** in the other boat to come and help them, and they came and filled boats so full that they began to sink. Then Jesus said to Simon, "Don't be afraid, from now on you will **fish for people**." Luke 5:5-7 & 10(NIV)*

It is always amazing to see how hard times have prepared us for expansion. The hard times will be a prelude for growth and our time of expansion. Achieving things in life and experiencing abundance will never replace the need to continue to pursue your purpose on a much deeper or expanded way. Do not settle; do not conclude your journey before the time. Be ready to walk away or even start again if necessary, but never get to a place where you settle or give up. Wait and pursue your promotion from "fish for fish" to "fish for people" promotion. Wait and pursue your time when the things that kept you in bondage (Peter always wanted to be the best fisherman) will have no hold on you and you can walk away from them to live a more expanded life.

People play such an important role in our lives. Even Peter needed partners to accomplish certain things in his life. However, when the expanded opportunity arrived, he decided to walk away from them to pursue his expansion. God knows what and whom you need as He calls you to an expanded life. There will be new people and new voices for your new season.

I lost my Dad who played such an important role in my life not so long ago. While I miss him, I miss nothing in my life. When I look around me, I have new people and new voices in my life that fulfill the role that my father used to play. My father was a great supporter of the call that God has over my life. With his departure, I have seen the increase of many more supporters; great men and women that are standing behind me. My Dad used to bring a great sense of humour and laughter to my family home, today my wife and daughters and even I sometimes play that role more so than in the past. The point I am making is this: do not let loss rob you of seeing God's provision over your life. Do not let loss rob you of seeing that God always provides what you need to complete your journey to the other side. You might be hanging out with a new crowd; with a new set of circumstances, but if you look carefully, you will realise that what you need is always available for you to continue your expanded life.

*Therefore, since we receive a **kingdom** which **cannot be shaken**, let us **show gratitude**, and offer to God pleasing service and acceptable worship with reverence and awe.*
- Hebrews 12:28 (AMP)

Saying thank you and living a life of gratitude will send out a loud message that you and I understand what we have received. There are certain things in our lives that cannot and will not be shaken. Our God-given purpose, destiny, and design submitted under His rule and governance cannot be shaken. Your outcome in the Lord is secured and guaranteed. Saying thank you for the small and big things in life will re-affirm your confidence in Him and shows that you acknowledge that God remains in charge. Saying "thank you" does something to God's heart. When you say "thank you", God is ready to bless you even more.

I see this with my daughters. Every time they say "Thank you" or show gratitude for what we do for them; great or small, we just want to do more for them. Gratitude allows God to spoil us with the necessary things that will expand our lives. Be on the lookout for moments and events where you can show gratitude to people around you. Look for opportunities where you can be of service to God; showing your gratitude to Him as you revere His grace over your life.

This reminds me of a time in my life where we lost everything we had. We were in serious debt and all our creditors were looking for us to settle our debt. It became so bad that we could not even afford milk to put into our tea or coffee or buy nappies for our kids. I remember getting up early one morning sitting on my *stoep* sipping on a cup of black coffee. While I was talking to God about our situation, His goodness overwhelmed me. I started to laugh, knowing that drinking black coffee or losing all our material things would not kill me, but that I do have everything I need to make a fresh start.

GETTING TO THE OTHER SIDE

That sense of deep gratitude started the flow of God's provision over our lives. Not long after that encounter, new job opportunities came our way and we could settle our debt in a very short space of time. Life did not return to normal. It returned to a better and brighter normal. Money never became an issue in our lives ever again as we continued to live a life of gratitude.

Expansion is available to everyone who is willing to venture into the deep to see life as an adventure where we overcome fictitious limitations and barriers, where we label loss as an opportunity to experience something new. It is a place where we see failure as our biggest opportunity to start again, just wiser; where we enjoy what we have and stop complaining about what we do not have, and where moving forward is a privilege and taking a pause is a luxury.

Do not be afraid of those who kill the body, but cannot kill the soul, but rather be afraid of Him who can destroy bought body and soul in hell - Matthew 10:28 (AMP)

Keep a balanced perspective in life. Protect what you think, how you feel, and how you make sense of the world. In most cases, your perspective in life will determine the outcome of your life.

It is time to wrap things up. What a journey; what a ride. As you make progress to the Other Side, do not forget that it always starts at a place of taking stock and having a clear vision of where you want to go. Once you do that, trust God to order your steps.

THANK YOU GOD FOR THIS AMAZING JOURNEY THAT YOU TOOK ME THROUGH!

ABOUT THE AUTHOR

Dean has committed himself to a journey of life-long learning and has read hundreds of books in his field of expertise, he has also obtained his Honors Degree in Human Resource Development from the University of Johannesburg, final year doing his Master's in Personal and Professional Leadership, Advance Management Program (AMP) from Duke University in the US, and an Executive Business and Digital Transformation Program from Duke CE SA where he is also part of the faculty. He has recently completed his Team Coaching Certification through METACO.

Dean has spent the last 10 years of his Corporate Career at Executive level scooping up the Chief Learning Officer Award for the country in 2014.

He brings genuine care and generosity to every engagement. He is a great sounding board and a critical and strategic thinker. He is an inspirational author and speaker and a credible builder of high-performing individuals, teams and businesses.

He embodies himself through:

The Leadership Storehouse - his own Leadership Development Firm that focuses on replenishing the "Soul" of a leader through speaking engagements, book launches, coaching and mentoring sessions and leadership seminars.

Ignite Family Church(IFC) - Where he plays the Lead Pastor role at the local Church in Eldorado Park that he co-founded. This is where he lives out his assignment to connect people to their God-given purpose, destiny and design. You can follow the work he does on the Facebook and Instagram pages of Ignite Family Church.

Retief Family - This is his most important "Brand" to uphold and maintain. Dean is married for 20 years to his University sweetheart - Samantha, Business Entrepreneur, Mrs SA Finalist 2018 and Women Empowerment winner, Women of Substance Finalist 2020, and co-lead Pastor of IFC. They have 2 lovely teenage daughters who are both inspirational in their own right. You can follow the family on Samantha Retief's Instagram page.

Dean can be contacted on:

Email: info@deanretief.co.za,
Linkedin: llinkedin.com/in/dean-retief-organisational-effectiveness-executive-partenr-123bb0a3,

Letter: Chapter 2

Notes

Writing a letter as opposed to just sitting down and thinking about your future will unleash your innermost emotions. Traumatic events coming out in the open will help you deal with them in a more positive way. This letter is private and for your eyes only, keep it in a safe place. You really need to be honest with yourself in this exercise, the deeper you can tap into your imagination and soul the more beneficial this letter will become.

Whilst writing your letter you need to concentrate on your emotions that drive you, these emotions are powerful motivating factors in your life.

Handwritten annotations:

- Pick up a journal
- Life Change Magazine
- I have taken golf
- Good time in the bush
- Life change seminar
- 4 Tribe
- looking natured and withdrawn
- 20 Coaches
- BOOK on
- New kid on the block

Handwritten letter:

Hi, I am / Dear, today is my 35th Birthday. I am glad to be alive, life has been good. God has been good. My wife and 2 children are experiencing life to the fullest (God) Useful healing / Articles. We have travelled into Europe / Africa / Asia. Financially independent and debt free. Community development Centre and Private business is thriving. Kids are well balanced, emotionally matured and gifted. Wife doing good counselling and child development. Marriage stable and meaningful / Intimate. Marriage Seminars etc. to example for others. I am the Pastor of a 2500 strong Church. Intense purpose driven. Influencing and developing new leaders / strong leaders / New leadership. I am in the process of writing my 1st book and being invited as a guest speaker at various functions nationally / internationally. I am physically and mentally fit. Parents are getting old but still alive. Own various properties X 3. 2 4X4's and 3 surfs in the boat → It is fun being alive !!!!

Hobbies: Birds, Farm, Horses, Ponies

www.ingramcontent.com/pod-product-compliance
Lightning Source LLC
Chambersburg PA
CBHW060528090426
42735CB00011B/2411